*To K,
I trust
back memories of bygone
days.*

NAKED EARS

A Child's-Eye View of the Great Depression

By

Altha Murphy

© 2002 by Altha Murphy. All rights reserved.

No part of this book may be reproduced, stored in a retrieval system, or transmitted by any means, electronic, mechanical, photocopying, recording, or otherwise, without written permission from the author.

ISBN: 1-4033-3062-X (e-book)
ISBN: 1-4033-3063-8 (Paperback)
ISBN: 1-4033-3064-6 (Dustjacket)

Library of Congress Control Number: 2002105741

This book is printed on acid free paper.

Printed in the United States of America
Bloomington, IN

1st Books - rev. 07/12/02

Table of Contents

IF A HOUSE COULD TALK	1
THE CLOSE CALLS	8
THE MONSTER	12
THE STRANGER	15
THE NEW SHOES	18
THE PRAYER	22
THE HAIR CUT	27
THE NAKED EARS	30
THE SHOPPING TRIP	34
THE CHRISTMAS PROGRAM	37
THE DINNER BUCKET	42
THE PLAYHOUSE	45
THE GAMES	49
THE ANKLETS	53
THE ARGUMENT	57
THE GHOST STORIES	62
THE FUNERAL	65
THE AUNT	69
THE OTHER AUNT	74
THE STORIES	77
THE HOG KILLING	81
THE BARN RAISING	85
THE SORGHUM MILL	89
THE REMEDIES	92
THE CREEPY CRAWLIES	97
THE FISH TRAP	101
THE CISTERN	104
THE RADIO	108
THE PETTICOAT	111
THE ORCHARD	116
THE PICTURE	120
THE SOUTHERN LADIES	125
THE APRON	129
THE MATTRESS	133
THE RECORD	136

THE SCARE	140
WASH DAY	145
IRONING DAY	148
THE BUTTER	152
THE SACKS	155
THE SPOOKY NIGHT	160
THE COUSINS	165
THE PERMANENT	169
THE TREATS	173
THE SAYINGS	176

IF A HOUSE COULD

Altha Murphy

Altha and her mother in front of the house in 1942 after it was remodeled.

The house as it looks today.

I'm a shambles now. My windows are broken, my ceiling is falling in, and my porches are all but gone. Tall grass and young cedar trees grow in my yard where flowers once bloomed. The cistern at my southeast corner, once so important, is boarded up and a tree grows from its opening.

Gone are the sounds of an active growing family which once echoed through my walls — the conversations, the laughter, the adolescent arguing, the sighings of contentment after a hard day's work. They are replaced by the wind groaning through my cracks. A

Naked Ears

family of mice scampers to their home in a pile of cotton they carried from an old couch.

But I have my memories; happy ones, sad ones, and everything in between. I remember when the man and his brother built me in the 1920s. They used board-and-batten for my outside walls which was wide oak planks with narrow slats to cover the cracks. I had four rooms, all floored with wide oak planks. But the front room was different. It had tongue-and-groove pine flooring over the oak planks.

I had a brick flue used for stoves in the front room and kitchen. My tin roof made for fine sleeping when the rain pattered down. Later, front and back porches were built, adding to my appearance and usefulness.

One day I was ready for the family to move into. How happy they were — the man, his wife, and two young sons, Millard and Volnia. Now the boys could walk a mile to the school. They had forty acres for clearing and growing crops. The family was grateful and content as they began life in a new community. They were proud of me, their brand new house!

Altha Murphy

I remember that October day, a year later, when the new baby came. Gertie, the woman, had told her friends she wanted a daughter and this time she got one. Neighbor women came to help and the boys were sent to visit their Uncle Charlie. Erastus, the man, hurried off to town to get the doctor. But that little miss was in a big hurry and arrived before the doctor did. Pearl, a sister-in-law, paced back and forth on my floor, wringing her hands. When she saw the doctor, she cried, "Doctor, get in here! That baby's already here!"

Unperturbed, he replied, "Now, just calm down, Mrs. Milgrim. That's what we want, isn't it?"

They named the baby Altha Verena. Her mother wanted to call her Verena, but her father said he would never be able to remember that name. So they called her Altha, although she sometimes went by the nicknames Punch and Scooter.

The next year saw the stock market crash, throwing the entire country into the Great Depression. Times were hard, but the family plugged on. They worked hard to make ends meet and never went hungry. At day's end they were glad to enter into my four walls for a good night's rest.

All three children completed the eighth grade at Annieville, a country school. Then they went on to complete high school in Imboden, a nearby town.

I remember the studying by kerosene lamplight, the stories the mother read to the family, and the chapters from the Bible. An oft-repeated phrase in her prayer was, "Lord, thank You that things are as well with us as they are."

Eventually Volnia and Altha married and left home, starting families of their own. Once again my walls echoed with laughter and childish activity as grandchildren were added to the family, then great grandchildren.

I could tell of good times and sad times within my walls. Times were good when neighbors helped each other as they did at our barn raising and at quilting parties. It's good to remember the meals of fresh fish from the pond, vegetables from the garden, and fruit from the orchard. When Altha's friends slept over, they talked and giggled into the night, sharing dreams and secrets.

Very seldom did they leave me alone. But once or twice a year the whole family loaded into the wagon and drove to visit Gertie's sister.

Her family had five youngsters, and with our three, there was plenty to talk about when they came home. Once the family went on an all-night fishing trip. I was lonely when everyone was gone, but listening to the excitement when they returned made up for it.

I got a facelift in the 1940s. By then my gray walls were looking drab. Erastus tore off my strips outside and decked me out in brick siding. He painted my facings white. Bright linoleum covered the floors. The boys were gone by then and Altha was the gofer. Hold this while I nail it. Sit on this board while I saw it. Hand me the hammer. What happened to that square? But she didn't mind, since her bedroom was fancied up along with the rest.

Life is a mixture of happiness and sorrow and my family had their share of sorrow. The 84-year-old grandmother died after living with them four years. At age seventeen Millard was struck with an illness which plagued him off and on the remainder of his life. It was sad when Volnia went into the armed services during World War II. He served in the Army Air Corps and was among the troops which invaded France on D-Day, June 6, 1944. Times were tense as they awaited news each day. But sadness turned into gladness when he returned safe and sound after the war was over.

Years later, it was sad when Erastus became unable to care for his farm, his cattle, and his orchard. Near the end of his life, he gave this bit of advice: "Don't get too comfortable in this world. Just when you think you've got it made, it will be time to leave."

I remember when the wife, children, and grandchildren, along with other relatives and friends, mourned his passing. Fifteen years later they said goodbye to the wife.

So here I stand, abandoned and desolate. No one has kept me repaired. I'm an eyesore to those who pass by.

The baby girl born on that October day has surpassed her allotted threescore and ten years. Each time she passes me, memories flood over her. She feels melancholy to see me in this condition. Then she remembers the good times, and she smiles. The stories which follow relate many of the memories she treasures of growing up within my four walls.

THE CLOSE CALLS

One could say it took a series of miracles to allow me to tell this story. When I was too young to remember, I had three close calls, either one of which could have proved fatal.

Two neighbor women told me that Mama was proud to have a little girl. She had three boys, but Alvin, the oldest, died as a baby. Several years after the three boys, I came along.

As I became older, I began helping with the housework. I learned about the close calls one day after we scrubbed the front room floor. Before cleaning the wood floor in a room, we took the furniture out or moved it around. We scrubbed the floor with a broom and soapy water. Then we rinsed it by pouring on plain water, swishing it around, and sweeping it out with the broom. After the floor dried, we put the furniture back in place.

That morning I noticed a funny-looking hole in the floor in the northwest corner of the front room. It was slanted and the planks were splintered around it. It didn't go through the wide oak planks on the bottom layer, just through the narrow pine ones on the top layer.

Naturally, my curiosity was aroused. "Mama, what is that place doing in the floor?" I asked. "I didn't know it was there."

"Oh, that happened when you were a baby," she said. Then she proceeded to tell me about that and the other close calls.

I learned that there were three incidents when my life could have ended, once as a baby and twice as a toddler. One Halloween night when I was a baby, a group of young people were making their rounds, playing pranks on neighbors. These were not children with trick-or-treat bags. They were teenagers and possibly some were young adults. It was commonplace for them to play harmful tricks, such as opening gates to turn livestock out.

My family members were in bed asleep when the pranksters came by. I was sleeping with my parents. Since our house had a tin roof, the young people thought it would be funny to throw rocks on it. They started out as gravel, then got larger and larger. A rock the size of a man's clenched fist crashed through the window and landed on the pillow inches from my head. Of course they ran when the heard the window glass break.

Scared and angry, Papa jumped out of bed, declaring that no one was going to "rock his kids." In the dark, he searched for his trusted squirrel gun, a 12 gauge shotgun. "I was begging him not to shoot," Mama said. "In his hurry to load the gun, it went off in the house. That's why that ugly place is in the corner. That's why we always keep a piece of furniture over it." Luckily, no one was injured that night.

The second close call came one day when Mama was preparing to churn. "I heated a dishpan of water and put it on the floor," she said "I turned to get the churn of milk to set in it. If the milk was warm the butter came faster. You saw the pan of water and must have thought it was bath time. You jumped right in it and scalded yourself. That was a scary time, but you got over it."

The third close call came one morning when the family was in the barn lot feeding the livestock and milking. I was supposed to stay in the house until they came in. Mama said, "I don't know what possessed you to go out to the lot that morning. You never had before. Maybe you got lonesome."

For whatever reason, I decided to join the family. Papa liked to break mules and we always had a pair named Jude and Kate. If he got rid of one, the next one would be either Jude or Kate. This particular Jude was mean. Just as I got inside the gate, he ran at me and lifted his hind feet to kick me. The family watched helplessly, unable to reach me, it happened so fast.

Mama said, "I never knew why, but just as Jude's feet would have hit your head, you squatted down real low on the ground and he missed you."

I had noticed that Mama always got a special kind of look when someone said something nice about her little girl. After we had that conversation while scrubbing the floor that morning, I began to understand why.

I'm glad I don't remember those times. Some things are best not remembered. But as an adult looking back, I feel there was divine intervention. For reasons of His own, God must have planned a long life for me.

THE MONSTER

I heard it before I saw it. What could that noise be? I was playing under the oak trees by the road. The closer it got, the more frightening it sounded. When it came into sight, I ran to safety in the house where Mama was washing dishes. "Mama, what is that horrible thing?" I asked. I had never seen or heard anything like it.

"Oh, that's a road grader," she said. "This is a county road and they grade it so it won't be so rough." She went on with her dish washing, just like it happened every day. She wasn't the least bit worried.

I was. Millard and Volnia had left for school a few minutes earlier. That monster was not far behind them, going the same way.

"But Mama," I said, "the boys just left. If that thing catches up with them, they won't have any place to go. It takes up the whole road and it will run over them."

"Oh, they'll be all right," she said as she stepped to the back door to throw the dish water out.

She made the beds and swept the floors. Then she sat down and unfastened her waist-length hair, combed it, braided it, and put it back up on the top of her head. How could she be so calm? Had she forgotten about the monster? I felt like tearing out on a shortcut through the fields and woods to warn my brothers to run for their lives. But she would see me and tell me to get back there, I might come up on a snake. Or the old bull might chase me in the pasture.

All day Mama went about her housework as if it were an ordinary day. Not me. I worried that the boys would never come home. Sometimes I didn't like the way they teased me, but I didn't want anything bad to happen to them.

Would that day never end? After we had eaten dinner, to keep my mind busy, I worked out a plan in my head. I had always called my brothers Muddie and Monnie. That's how I said their names when I first began talking, and I had never bothered to try to pronounce them correctly. What if they did come home, and what if I could say their names? Wouldn't they think that was something? So I practiced. And I practiced. By mid-afternoon, I announced to Mama, "I can say Muddie's and Monnie's names. Listen. Mil-lard. Vol-nee. Mill-ard. Vol-nee. I said them several times and she thought it was good.

I didn't mention the monster to her again, but that was the longest afternoon I had ever seen. I kept my eyes glued to the gravel road in the direction they left that morning, all the while repeating, "Mil-lard. Vol-nee." About four-thirty they came into sight, as they did each school day. They looked just like they did when they left that morning, carrying their books and swinging their dinner buckets.

Wonderful! Somehow they had escaped being taken down by the monster. Just wait till I spring my surprise on them. They will be so proud of me. I met them at the yard gate. "Guess what! Listen to this. Mil-lard. Vol-nee." I repeated it a few times in case the significance of the moment had not soaked in. They looked at me and nodded. That was it! They nodded! Then they wanted to know what was for supper.

What did it matter? I had accomplished something and my brothers were safe. I wouldn't even mind a little teasing now. The day didn't turn out so bad, after all.

THE STRANGER

Later I would learn that this was the Great Depression. At the time I only knew that I spent the long hot summer days playing with my dog, the cats, and a doll Mama made for me the past Christmas.

One hot day a stranger came to our door. After introducing himself, he said that he owned horses which his cowhands were bringing through the country. He asked, "Could I stay with you until they catch up with me? Could you keep my horses in your pasture a day or two when they get here?"

We took the stranger in and treated him as one of the family. In those days people didn't turn anyone from their door without helping to meet a need.

The first night he had wonderful news. "Since you are so kind, I have a Shetland pony I will give to your little girl." My heart raced. I could hardly believe it. A pony all my own! What a wonderful man!

The next morning the stranger went out to the road. Shading his eyes with his hand, he looked toward the east. He strained to see if he could hear the horses' hooves clip-clopping on the gravel road.

"Nothing yet," he said. "Well, tomorrow for sure." That meant I would have to wait another day to see my pony.

This happened day after day. Each time Papa asked. "Any sign of them yet?"

"No, I don't understand what could be holding them up. They're never more than a day or two behind me. They must have had trouble."

Each night after supper was over, this man sat with us in the front room and told interesting stories about his life. He took me on his lap and talked about my pony.

By now I was getting so anxious to see the pony I couldn't sleep for a long time after I went to bed. I could just imagine the little fellow, no taller than myself, carrying me around over the fields. "I'll keep you brushed and shiny," I promised him. "I'll let my friends ride you, because not one of them has a pony. I must think of a special name for you. Not just any old name will do for a pretty pony like you." On and on I went, finally talking myself to sleep, certain that tomorrow would be the day.

Several days passed and no horses had arrived. One morning I heard Papa say, "If that man had any horses, they would be here by now." My heart sank. If there were no horses, did that mean no pony?

The stranger must have known the family was getting suspicious, since he left suddenly without an explanation. No horses! There never had been any horses. No pony! There had never been a pony.

There would be many disappointments awaiting me in life. But that was the first one I remember, and I was crushed. I couldn't understand why this man would promise me a pony when he didn't have one.

I heard the grownups talking about hard times and that everyone finds a way to survive. Papa said, "That must be the way he gets by. He has a place to sleep and three meals a day till a family finds him out. Then he moves on to another community."

After the stranger left we heard that he had done a family in another community the same way. Yes, they had a little girl and, yes, he promised her a Shetland pony.

THE NEW SHOES

Cotton picking time was a fun time, at least for me. I was too little to pick, so I spent the day playing while the others worked. The wagon had sideboards and was parked at the end of the field just across the fence from a neighbor's yard. Old Jack, our dog, went to the field with us and stayed near me. He slept in the shade a lot.

That afternoon the wagon was almost filled with cotton. My parents and brothers had long sacks with straps which went over their shoulders. They went up and down the rows picking the cotton from bolls and putting it into the sacks. When the sacks were full, they weighed them and dumped the cotton into the wagon. Their fingers got sore from the pointed ends of the dried bolls. But that was to be expected. Everyone got sore hands when picking cotton.

I spent a lot of time climbing in and out of the wagon and playing in the soft fluffy cotton. When I became tired, I just took myself a nap.

Papa planted watermelons in some of the rows. I liked it when someone came upon a ripe melon. He burst it into red juicy chunks and we all sat on the sacks and ate it. Who cared if the juice ran down our chins?

There were trees nearby with ripe red delicious apples. I could get an apple any time I wanted.

Sometimes I went over the fence into the neighbor's yard to play. Mrs. Dutton always came out to talk when she saw me. She didn't have children of her own, and she lived alone, so she probably enjoyed the conversation, even if half of it was childish. She usually served bread and jam when little ones came to visit.

I knew that Papa got money for the cotton when he took it to the gin. He let me go along and ride on top. But I had to sit in the middle and sit still so I wouldn't fall off. The old bumpy road didn't seem rough with all that cotton underneath me. Coming home in the empty wagon was a different story. He liked to have a load which would make a five-hundred-pound bale. I felt that tomorrow he would be going to the gin at Ravenden.

That morning I had a super idea. I would love to have a new pair of shoes. I didn't care nearly as much for dresses and other clothes as

I did shoes. But Papa had already said, "You don't need new shoes, because the ones you have are not worn out."

I knew he was right, that the old shoes did have some wear left in them. I got them in the spring, but had gone barefooted a lot that summer. New shoes were bought with space in the toes for "growing room." So I pouted a bit. I had a habit of sticking my lower lip out when I was unhappy. Mama didn't like that, so I tried to do it when she wasn't looking. I still hadn't figured out how she saw me the last time I tried it, because she was stirring the lye soap in the iron kettle in the back yard. The slap I received was a reminder not to do it around her, even if her head was turned. I had decided mamas must be able to see things the rest of us couldn't.

So there I sat on the cotton, thinking and pouting. If I didn't have those old shoes, I could get a new pair. There was no way I could wear them out that day, even if I ran and jumped and climbed till sundown. Suddenly a light came on. I took off those old shoes, stood up straight, and slung them, one at a time, as far as I could send them. They landed in the weeds near the apple tree.

When my folks got to the end of the rows and came to weigh up, I yelled, "Look, I don't have any shoes!" They looked and, sure enough, I was as barefooted as Old Jack.

It took those big brothers of mine about two minutes to find the shoes. Why must they be so helpful? As they held the shoes up, everyone looked at each other, then at me. I was waiting for the other shoe to drop, so to speak. Would I get a dose of Mama's "peach tree tea," or worse still, a talk from Papa? But he surprised everyone by saying, "If that kid wants a pair of new shoes that bad, we'll just buy her a pair."

How lucky could a girl get? Tomorrow I wouldn't mind coming home on the bumpy road in the empty wagon at all. A pair of shiny new shoes could smooth out rough places as nothing else could.

THE PRAYER

Whew! That was a close call! I hope I never get in a jam like that again.

The time was the early 30s. It began as I played under the two big oak trees between our front yard and the road. During hot weather I spent a lot of time playing there in the shade.

A car had been under the trees a few days. A Whippet, they called it. It belonged to Mr. Byron Marshall, the man who owned the ground we rented. We had forty acres of our own, but that wasn't enough to support a family of five.

My folks were considering buying the car, so Mr. Marshall left it there a few days while they made the decision. We had never owned a car. Millard and Volnia were hoping we took it. I tagged along behind them a lot and had heard them talk while they milked the cows. "Wouldn't it be fine if we had a car?" asked Millard.

"It sure would," said Volnia. "We either have to walk everywhere we go, or if the whole family goes, we have to take time to hitch the team. We could be where we're going by the time we do that." So they milked, and they dreamed. I dreamed, too. I wanted us to buy the car.

Earlier that afternoon, I checked to see if anyone happened to be watching. No one was, so I opened a door and hopped in the back seat. Just to get the feel of it in case we did buy it. The seat was all clean and soft, and ever so comfortable. Turning around, I noticed a window shade on the back window. Hm-m-m, that was interesting. It had fringe on the bottom and a little ring to put your finger in. I wasn't familiar with window shades. Our windows in the house had curtains made of sacks, starched and ironed, but no shades. I gave the tiniest yank. The shade moved down a bit and stopped. That was fun! One more little pull couldn't possibly hurt anything, could it?

After a few more little tugs, the shade plopped all the way down, even past the bottom of the window and onto the back seat. Oh, my! I wasn't prepared for that. I would have to give it a sharp pull and let it fly back up. Even after several sharp pulls, it didn't move one inch.

Now it was time to worry. What if the shade never went back up? What kind of trouble would I be in then? Mama would give me a dose of her peach tree tea, swats across the bare legs with a little peach tree branch. Worse still, Papa might give me one of his talks. And Mr.Marshall, what would he do? I wondered if they put kids in jail for stuff like this. I had never heard of one being jailed. But then, I had also never heard of a kid ruining someone else's car.

I thought maybe I should pray about it. I had heard Mama sing a song as she worked about a royal telephone. It went something like this:

> Central's never busy, always on the line.
> You can hear from heaven almost any time.
> Built by God the Father for His very own,
> You can talk to Jesus on this royal telephone.

I felt a need to use that telephone, but I only knew one prayer. I said it each night before I went to bed. It went like this:

> Now I lay me down to sleep.
> I pray the Lord my soul to keep.
> If I should die before I wake,
> I pray the Lord my soul to take.

I wasn't excited about the part that talked about dying before I wake. But that's how the prayer went, so that's what I said.

We had a big picture on the wall over my bed with a little boy and his dog kneeling by his bed, saying their prayers. I wondered if that boy said the same prayer I did each night.

At any rate, I didn't feel that prayer fit the predicament I found myself in with the shade. So I forgot about rhyming words and memorized lines. I began talking directly to God, begging Him to get me out that mess, and to please hurry, before I got caught. I promised Him if He would make that window shade go up, I would do anything He wanted me to do.

When I finished talking on the royal telephone, I gave the shade one more yank. Miracle of miracles, it rolled up on that roller and snapped into place as if it had always been there. I got out of the car and shut the door. No one could tell by looking that I had been in it.

That night at supper Papa had an announcement. "I don't think we will take the car. We just can't afford it now." My brothers looked at each other, disappointment written on their faces, but they didn't say anything.

At that point, I didn't even care. I was so relieved that my prayer had been answered, I didn't care if I had to walk everywhere I went

Altha Murphy

from that day forward. No one knew I had been fooling around where I had no business. No one, that is, except God — and He wasn't telling!!!!

THE HAIR CUT

I had never seen my papa that angry before. I didn't ever remember hearing him and Mama having a big argument. It really wasn't much of an argument this time. It was one-sided, because she wasn't saying much. He was ranting and raving and she was listening.

Mama had black hair when she was young. She was thirty-three when I was born and her hair was already white. She was eight years younger than Papa, but some folks thought she was older, all because of her white hair. I had seen a picture of her when she was young and she looked pretty with the black hair. Just the same, I liked her with white hair. People talked about her beautiful hair and it made me proud. Her hair was thick and silky and until that day had come down to her waist. She braided it and wrapped the braids on top of her head. It took a long time to wash and dry it. It even took a long time to comb it and put it up each morning. In the summer when she cooked and canned at the kitchen stove, it became sweaty and stuck to her head.

That morning Mama was ready for a change. After Papa left the house, she went to see her neighbor and good friend, Myrtle Reed.

She asked Myrtle to cut her hair. There was a drastic change after the hair cut. Now it came just below the ears. I did a double-take the first time I looked at it. It would take some getting used to. But I thought if she wanted short hair, so be it.

When Papa came home, the fireworks started. He took one look at her and stormed, "What have you done to yourself?"

"Well, I got a hair cut," she replied with surprising calmness.

A lot of people believed it was sinful for a woman to have short hair because the Bible says that a woman's hair is her glory. Apparently Papa was one of those people.

Then he used sarcasm, which was out of character for him. "You don't have the shame of an old sheep dog. If you shear a sheep dog, he will crawl under something to hide because he's ashamed to be seen. You're standing there for everyone to see. Why didn't you say something before I left this morning?"

"Because you wouldn't have wanted me to do it, and I wanted my hair cut. I was tired of it being so long."

I was uncomfortable with the scene. I didn't like what I was hearing. But if I knew my papa, he would be angry and hurt for a while. Then, because he couldn't change it, he would make the best of it. He would say what he had to say then and not keep throwing it up to her.

From that day forward, Mama had short hair. I never heard Papa mention it again.

THE NAKED EARS

I knew I must be different from everyone else, but I didn't understand why. I looked closely at everyone I was around, paying special attention to their ears. I couldn't tell that they were a lot different from mine, but I knew they had to be.

You see, I had naked ears. We pronounced it "nekked." I knew this because each time I washed, Mama said, "Be sure to wash your naked ears."

We were in the middle of the Great Depression, but I didn't know what that meant. My friends and relatives lived the same way we did, and I didn't remember when times had been better.

We lived in a four-room house on a forty-acre farm in the foothills of the Ozark Mountains. We had a front room, a kitchen, a bedroom, and a "junk room." Porches were on the front and back of the house.

The kitchen contained the wood cook stove which served many purposes. It cooked our food, kept it warm, kept the water hot, and provided warmth for bath taking in cold weather.

Each time I bathed, I scrubbed and rinsed and dried until my ears were rosy red. Without fail, Mama always asked, "Did you wash your naked ears?"

"Yes, Mama, I did," I always answered.

"Did you do a good job of it?" she wanted to know.

"Yes, Mama, I did a good job." Sometimes, just to be sure, she checked.

I didn't know why my ears were naked, but if Mama said they were, that settled it. My hair came down over my ears, so you couldn't see them, except the tips. I saw men and boys, even Papa and my brothers, going around with their ears just sitting on the sides of their heads, completely uncovered. I noticed that many women, including Mama, wore their hair up so their whole ears showed. But Mama never called their ears naked, just mine.

I suppose I could have asked her why it was only my ears that were naked, and no one else's, but I never did. She probably didn't know why, and I was afraid she might be embarrassed because she had the only kid in the country with naked ears.

This had gone on each time I bathed as long as I could remember. I felt sure that when I was too young to bathe myself, she had seen to it that the ears were taken care of.

She probably didn't know this, but she didn't need to remind me each time. Since my ears were naked, everyone would be looking at them. It was bad enough to have naked ears. I most certainly would not be caught with *dirty* naked ears.

That morning began like all the others, with me bathing in the kitchen, paying special attention to—you guessed it—my naked ears. Mama called from the front room, "Did you wash your neck and ears?"

What was that? Was she saying what I thought she was? I had to hear that again. "What did you say?" I shouted through the closed door.

She answered, "I just asked if you washed your neck and ears."

I couldn't believe my naked ears! I heard her correctly the first time. Relief flooded over me like bath water running down. All this time she hadn't been saying my ears were naked. She just wanted to make sure my neck and ears were clean.

After basking in the intense relief for a few minutes, I began considering another matter. While putting so much time and effort into cleaning my ears, was there a possibility I could have been neglecting my neck?

Altha Murphy

THE SHOPPING TRIP

A special day like that came along only once a year. It was special because I was going shopping with Papa. We were not going to the neighborhood store, but all the six miles into Imboden. Christmas was approaching and I could feel it in the air.

I didn't have to be called to breakfast that morning. I was up early and raring to go. It would be just the two of us and I had an important job. When we went down the big hill, I would hold the brake on the wagon. I ate my bowl of rice and my biscuit with chocolate gravy in a hurry and waited with excitement while Papa harnessed Jude and Kate to the wagon.

I didn't know what we would buy that day. It would probably be flour, beans, sugar, and coffee and maybe some feed for the livestock. But I knew Mama had made a list so she could make goodies for the holidays. We always got apples, oranges, candy, nuts, and a coconut or two for Christmas. The list might contain bananas and raisins for baking.

I didn't know if there would be a gift that year. I knew there wasn't a Santa Claus. My parents didn't believe in telling a child there was one, as that would not be truthful. Some of my friends believed in Santa, and I didn't burst their bubbles by blabbing. I would get something if there were enough money. One year Mama made me a doll with pretty clothes. Another year I got a shiny new red wagon. Half the fun was watching Papa and the boys put it together.

Gift or not, Christmas would be special. There would be a program at school. Our relatives would visit, bringing my cousins. We would play till we were drop-dead tired, then go in and stuff ourselves with food on that loaded dining table.

When we got to town and went into Matthews' store, I could hardly believe all the things for sale. There were groceries and clothes for everyone. There were toys, candy, and fruit. I walked down the aisles on wood floors and gazed into the glass showcases.

As I stood admiring the trinkets in the showcases, Papa came by. He gave me some money and told me to pick out something I liked. I counted the coins and there were four dimes. That was forty cents. Now I had big decisions to make.

After looking everything over a few times, I selected my treasures. I chose a string of beads, a picture in a frame, a purse, and a pretty handkerchief. Each cost a dime and that made forty cents exactly.

Since December days are short, it was almost dark when we got home. I was tired and went to bed after supper. But sleep didn't come right away. Visions danced in my head: a vision of the picture hanging on the wall; a vision of how I would look in church Sunday with beads around my neck; a vision of what it would be like to carry a new purse with a pretty embroidered hanky with lace tucked inside; a vision of relatives visiting; a vision of me saying my piece at the Christmas program; a vision of that table loaded with Christmas goodies.

I hadn't slept much the night before, looking forward to the trip into town. The day had brought almost more excitement than I could handle. Finally, exhaustion overtook me. As I drifted off to sleep, I thought this would have to be the best Christmas a girl ever had.

THE CHRISTMAS PROGRAM

The Milgrim family, 1933
Seated, left to right: Erastus, Altha, Gertie
Standing, left to right: Volnia, Millard

The pie supper always came before the Christmas program. Women and girls baked pies, put them in decorated boxes, and took them to the schoolhouse to be auctioned off. Men and boys bid on the pies, and each ate with the one whose pie he bought. If a guy were sweet on a girl, the other males made it difficult for him by running up the price of the pie. He would know which box was hers, since he had brought her to the pie supper, or she had let him know. When he began bidding, the others also knew. He might have to pay two or three dollars, while the other pies went for fifty or seventy-five cents.

Contests were held to determine the prettiest girl and the ugliest man. Two or three people were nominated for each honor, and the winners were those who had the most money put on them. The prizes were a cake for the beauty and a jar of sour pickles for the less fortunate one. This was all done in fun, however, since everyone knew the money would be used for treats at the Christmas program.

Treats were only part of the Christmas program. Students presented a play, sang carols, and did recitations. They worked for weeks in advance to present the perfect program. The entire community turned out for the big night.

The first program I remember was when I was in first grade. I was only four the previous summer when I coaxed my parents into letting me visit the first day of school with my two big brothers. They were both in seventh grade, and I sat between them in their double seat. I liked it so much I cried to go back the second day, and the third, and the fourth. Mr. Lloyd Reed was a neighbor and family friend who taught grades one through eight. He said to my parents, "Why don't you let her start? She can learn and I don't mind a bit." That settled it.

We went to school in July and August, after the cotton was laid by. That meant all the chopping and plowing was completed, and the cotton plants were given time to mature and produce. September and October were vacation months so students could pick cotton and help harvest other crops. Also, wood had to be cut for the winter. School began again in November and lasted five or six more months, depending on how the money held out to pay the teacher.

A few days before the program, teacher and students went into the surrounding woods to cut a big cedar tree. On Friday night it stood in the corner of the classroom, decorated with paper chains, strings of popcorn and strings of red berries. In Arkansas, small bushes are loaded with bright red berries in the winter months. No one seems to know their name, but they were easy to string and they added color to the tree.

Brown bags were plentiful underneath the tree on that special night. Each contained an apple, an orange, candy, and nuts. Each person received a bag, adults as well as children. We had practiced on the program until Mr. Reed felt we had it right. Older children were in the play, while younger ones said poems. Everyone, including the audience, sang the carols.

I knew my poem like the back of my hand. I was dressed in my best dress, long stockings, and new patent leather shoes.

The stage went across the front of the classroom, and wires near the ceiling partitioned it into three sections. Sheets, which served as curtains, were fastened to the wires with huge safety pins. Two big boys pulled them back and forth along the wires. We waited in the left section until our turn, then entered into the midsection to perform, then exited into the right section to wait for the program to end.

I could hardly wait until my turn came. Just wait till the people saw me in my good dress and new shoes! Back went the curtains and I found myself on the stage alone. I looked out and saw a sea of people out there, every one of them looking directly at me. My knees began to shake and, worse than that, my mouth wouldn't work. I tried, but not a sound came out. My throat was dry as cotton and a big knot lodged in my throat. Mr. Reed whispered from behind the curtain, "Roses...." Nothing happened.

He tried again, "Go ahead, Altha, say your piece. Roses on my...."

He waited and waited. Finally, he said to the boys, "She's not going to say it. You might as well pull the curtains."

Slowly, the curtains started moving. How terrible! I just had to get my mouth working. As the curtains came closer and closer together, the words started coming out, almost tumbling over each other:

> Roses on my shoulder
> Slippers on my feet.
> I'm Papa's curly-headed baby
> Don't you think I'm sweet?

I finished just before the curtains closed in front of me. The people must have liked it, because they all laughed and clapped. I felt so proud. I had really done it—my very first performance.

THE DINNER BUCKET

Ah, what goodies that dinner bucket held. I walked a mile to school in the 1930s, but some children had to walk much farther. After walking to school early in the morning, working hard on reading and arithmetic and all the other subjects during "books," and playing hard at recess, everyone was ready to dive into that dinner bucket at noon.

The bucket was usually a lard bucket or syrup bucket with a tight lid. If two or more children were from the same family, they might share an eight-pound lard bucket, or they could use more than one bucket. If a family only had one child, a four-pound bucket would do.

We had two months of summer school, then we were out two months for fall harvest and wood cutting. Then it was back to school for five or six months. That meant we were in school the hottest and coldest seasons of the year.

The dinner bucket held many different foods. There were sandwiches, all made with biscuits. Bought "light bread" was a luxury to be enjoyed on special occasions, such as when your papa brought home a pound of bologna. A biscuit might hold a fried egg, butter and jelly, fried ham, or fried sausage. Sometimes it held fried potatoes. To this day I still like cold fried potatoes. Summer months allowed for fresh fruit and vegetables. Any time of year one might have a boiled egg or two. Almost always there was something sweet in the bucket. Mama made me butter rolls and chocolate rolls. She fried pies with raisins or dried peaches or dried apples. A bucket might hold cake, cookies, or canned fruit in a glass jar.

Two long handmade benches sat at the back corner of the classroom. One held two water buckets, each with a dipper. When we arrived in the morning, we lined our dinner buckets on that bench. If we needed more space, we used the second one.

At times we gathered in small groups to eat. At other times we all ate together. We had to get the food down fast, since we only had an hour for noon. We couldn't afford to miss any precious play time.

When the weather was warm, we gathered under the trees on the playground to eat. In cold weather, we ate around the potbellied stove in the center of the room. Everyone checked out what the others had in their buckets. Quite often, some swapping took place. That way we could determine who were the best cooks in the community. After all, we frequently spent the night with a friend. If it happened to be a friend whose mama was a good cook, so much the better.

Nothing kept us from getting into the buckets at first recess if we felt the need for a snack. There was also no law against saving something for last recess or to munch on the way home. Most families didn't eat supper until the night chores were done. It was a long time from noon to that meal, especially in the summer.

Two things stand out in my memory. First, almost every bucket was empty at the end of the day. Second, I do not recall hearing anyone complain about the food.

THE PLAYHOUSE

This was the Annieville schoolhouse. A church met in the building on Sundays and this is a picture of a church gathering on an Easter Sunday. The building was built by Oddfellows lodge members as a lodge hall. They met in the upper story and school was held on the ground floor. Years when there were enough students for two teachers, both stories were used for classrooms.

We worked hard all week cleaning, sweeping, and carrying rocks. We built a playhouse at school which we planned to use for a long time. We each had a playhouse at home, but it was more fun to have one at school, since so many playmates were there. We searched high and low for treasures to put in the playhouse.

We attended a country school, and that particular year one teacher taught grades one through eight. Woods surrounded the playground and we found the ideal spot in the edge of the trees. We were there before school and at each recess, morning, noon, and afternoon, busy as bees.

We used branches with leaves on them for brooms to sweep away sticks and other trash. We made the walls with rows of rocks. This house had three rooms, a front room, a kitchen, and a bedroom. Cushions of moss lying by the trees made nice beds and chairs. We brought broken dishes and old pans and tall sticks from home.

Little girls in school were our daughters, and they delighted in their roles. However, not even the smallest boys could be coaxed into being our sons. No, Siree! They would not be caught dead playing in an old playhouse with girls. They were not sissies! We knew this influence came from the older boys, since the small boys sometimes played with their sisters in playhouses at home. Because we were helpless to change the situation, that's where the tall sticks came into play. We used them for our husbands and sons. It worked pretty well, too, because there was never any male back talk.

What a bunch of busy mommies we were. There was only one drawback. Just as our involvement became intense in building or playing, the school bell rang. Then we had to drop everything and go inside to do reading or arithmetic or something else. But as soon as the teacher announced, "You're dismissed for recess," we tore out again for the playhouse.

Only two things in school were as much fun as recess. Almost every Friday after last recess, we had a ciphering match. Two big kids were named team leaders. They chose the other students, one at a time, until everyone was on a team. Each child waited with anxiety, whispering a little prayer, "Please don't let me get picked last." One from each team stood at the blackboard—yes, it really was black—and did an arithmetic problem which the teacher called out. The first one to get the correct answer and call it out won, and the opposing team member sat down. The last one standing determined the winning team. Occasionally we had a spelling match instead.

The other fun thing to do was to carry drinking water. The teacher sent two boys or two girls, each with a ten quart bucket, to the Evergreen well a quarter of a mile away. Each bucket held a dipper, so we could get the first cold drink after it was drawn. Those chosen for this task were allowed to go during "books," thus evading some study time. Books was the opposite of recess.

We completed the playhouse on a Friday. We played in it only a short while at last recess. That day my team won the ciphering match, so all weekend I felt good about things in general. Monday would be a good day.

Monday was not a good day. When we rushed out to the playhouse before school, a disaster awaited us. Everything was a big mess. Dishes and pans were strewn all over the place, even outside the rock walls. The walls had been kicked around till we couldn't tell where the rooms had been outlined. Sticks and trash littered the once-clean floor.

We didn't tattle. What would have been the use, without proof? But we knew. Oh, we knew, all right. All we could do was go back into the classroom and mutter, "Stinkin' old boys!" under our breath each time we came near each other.

THE GAMES

What did we do in our spare time? We found plenty to do when we didn't have to work.

We played indoor and outdoor games at home and at school. Few games could be played indoors at school. Each Friday after last recess, we had a ciphering match or a spelling match. When it was raining or very cold, we moved the desks and benches around to make a big open space. We played blindfold, fruit-basket-upset, Jacob and Rachel, or hot potato.

We had more choices for outdoor games at school. Children and young people of all ages attended Annieville School. At times we all played together. At other times the younger ones might play drop the handkerchief, rotten egg, tag, Mother, may I? New Orleans, hopscotch, or jump rope. The girls played house, while the boys shot marbles. Special marbles were a source of pride and to be protected at all costs.

All of us were likely to join in a game of hide and seek, run sheep run, wolf over the river, ante over, three deep, flying Dutchman, skip to my Lou, or pop the whip. Pity the poor soul on the end of the whip if the line was long. Usually a ball game was going on with lots of whooping and hollering.

It was even possible to have fun on the way to and from school. If you could get a Prince Albert tobacco can, you could nail the middle of it to a stick and bend the ends out. Then you could roll a metal hoop all the way to school and back. Some kids were so good at this they could go the whole distance without losing the hoop once.

During the winter, when the ice was thick, we skated on the Evergreen pond. This was usually on the way home, since few of us got started early enough in the mornings.

If you had time, you could find plenty of fun things to do at home. Girls could spend days with a Sears Roebuck catalog. Besides looking and wishing, there was the world of paper dolls. They could cut out whole families, mamas and papas, grandmas and grandpas, boys, girls, and babies. The stiff backs of catalogs were fine for making furniture like beds, tables, chairs, and stoves. All this could be stored in boxes, and shoved under the bed to be retrieved at a later time.

Other indoor games included dolls, jacks, dominoes, checkers, jigsaw puzzles, I spy, and riddle-me-riddle-me-ree. Mama made us a fox and goose board. We used a button for the fox and corn for the geese.

Outdoor games at home included some of the ones we played at school. Others were horseshoes, see-saw, and jump-the-board. That one could be dangerous if you didn't watch where your feet landed.

Sometimes we made up games. My friend Anna Beth and I made up one we called kill. We stood facing each other at a distance and threw a coke bottle. When the bottle left our hand, we yelled, "Kill." The other one fell before the bottle landed. Once she wasn't looking and didn't fall. After the bottle hit her, she ran into the house, crying, with a big knot on her head. I ran home as fast as my legs would carry me. Mama didn't know about it until a few days later when she saw Anna Beth's mama. I just knew they would both be mad at me, but they weren't. Guess they thought it was an accident, but they put a stop to our little game.

In winter we skated on the pond. When it snowed, we had snowball fights and made snow angels.

On Sundays a mama never knew how many she was cooking for. Her children might bring friends home from church. Or a whole family might go home with another family. When that happened, there were always games in the afternoon. The men joined the youngsters in pitching horseshoes or playing ball while the women sat and talked.

Young people liked to go to Broadway's and ride the flying jenny. This was a log centered on a stump and fastened so it turned. It was fun to watch, but I was too scared to ride. Once Volnia got knocked down with it when his head was turned.

I only remember two store bought toys. Relatives in Illinois sent me a doll one Christmas. Another year my family gave me a red wagon. But we entertained ourselves just fine. The only problem was we felt that there was too much work and not enough time for play.

THE ANKLETS

I used to wonder why I couldn't be like other girls. Why did I have go around looking like Old Mother Hubbard? Other girls my age wore anklets to school and their legs were bare in cold weather. They didn't come down with some dreaded disease, but seemed to be as healthy as I was.

Perhaps it was because my parents were older than those of most of my friends. I regarded them as super old fashioned. They thought I would take pneumonia, or at least catch a death of cold, if I went bare legged, as they called it.

So I trudged off to school each morning with not only long stockings, but also with long handles underneath them. The stockings were tan with a ribbed texture. They came up above my knees, and were secured with, of all things, rubber garters made from strips of old inner tube. We didn't own a car, so I don't know where Mama got the worn out inner tube. But she managed. My dress came below my knees, so at least the garters were hidden from sight.

The cuffs on the bottom of the legs of the long handles were always stretched. So each morning I went through the same ritual: lap the cuffs over at the bottom; pull those old tan stockings over them all the way up past my knees; secure them with the rubber garters. It was impossible to accomplish this without the folds in the cuffs showing. I didn't want anyone to know I wore long underwear, but there they were in plain sight, the telltale bulges at the ankles.

The garters were tight. They had to be to hold up all that mess. Mama kept her stockings up by tying narrow strips of material below her knees. That would never work for me with all the running and jumping which took place at recess. Also, when the ice was thick enough on the Evergreen pond, we children stopped and skated a while on the way home from school. String garters would never have withstood that activity.

At that point in my life I was beginning to notice that boys were looking a bit interesting. Before, I had regarded them as a necessary evil, or at the least, pests to be endured or ignored. For many years I had been one of the smaller girls at our school. I had never completely forgiven the boys for tearing our playhouses down almost as fast as we built them. By now some of the older children, including my brothers, had left and I was an upper grade student. The world was taking on a new perspective. But who would look twice at a girl bundled up like a grandma?

I knew there was no changing my parents. If anything changed, it would be up to me. I had heard that necessity was the mother of invention, but hadn't thought about what it meant until then.

Necessity was staring me in the face. I must no longer look like someone from that history book in my desk. Could I invent a plan that would make me look more modern?

Anklets were out of the question. I knew not to ask. One morning I dressed in the usual attire and began the mile long walk to school. After passing the Dutton house, I stopped in the middle of the gravel road. I took those rubber garters off and stuffed them in my coat pockets. I rolled those ugly tan stockings in neat little folds down to my shoe tops. I rolled those tacky long handle legs in neat little folds up past my knees so my dress would cover them.

I didn't exactly make a fashion statement that day. I didn't look like the other girls, but I was bare legged throughout the day. That afternoon I stopped at the same spot and put everything back in place before coming into sight of our house.

I didn't come down with pneumonia or a cold the next day, so I kept on with the routine. Most days went smoothly after that, except when the games got extra lively at recess. If that happened, I felt a need to monitor and adjust. However, that was no problem. I could just sidle over to that little house in the edge of the woods marked GIRLS and make the necessary adjustments. No one was the wiser.

I knew I was supposed to obey my parents, and I did. After all, neither of them had ever told me *not* to roll my stockings down or my underwear up!

THE ARGUMENT

The quiet summer day suddenly became anything but. Grandma was yelling in the kitchen, giving someone "what for." I had to go see what the excitement was about.

Grandma was eighty when she came to live with us. She had raised four sons of her own and three grandchildren. She was a tiny woman, stooped from the waist. She was crippled, having had white swelling when she was young. One of her feet drew up so she walked on her toes on that foot. I had no idea what white swelling was, but if it did that to your foot, I didn't ever want it. She walked with a cane. Someone had whittled it from wood. Instead of having a crook on top, it had a ball which fitted into her hand. She didn't call it a cane; it was her walking stick, or usually just her stick.

My favorite piece of furniture was a rocking chair Papa bought for me at a sale. Grandma fit right into my chair, so I had to share it with her. But I didn't mind. I wasn't in the house nearly as much as she was.

Grandma was Cherokee Indian, either full or half. I don't know which. I didn't ask when I was young and now everyone is gone who would know. She was reared by her grandmother, who was reported to be a medium. She could tell ghost stories that made me so scared I sometimes was afraid to sleep at night.

She had not had an easy life. Her husband had died, leaving three young sons. Two of those sons died at a young age. When Mabel, the granddaughter whom she had reared, married at age sixteen, she moved in with us. She was a little girl during the Civil War. Sometimes her mind played tricks on her and she thought the soldiers were coming. She called Papa by her brother's name and wanted us all to hide so they couldn't find us. But usually her mind was clear and we understood why she had those bad times.

It must have been hard on her, having so much idle time on her hands after being busy all those years. She liked to wash dishes, but couldn't see well enough to get them clean. She was unable to do any kind of needlework.

After she had been with us two years, something happened which she saw as an opportunity to be in charge again. Mama and her sister, my Aunt Zona, found their brother, my Uncle Albert, after several years of not knowing his whereabouts. They got so excited they hopped on a train and went all the way to Keiser to visit him for a week. Where in the world was Keiser? It sounded like it could be on the other side of the world.

Mama had never left us before. It seemed strange without her. But she arranged for our care while she was gone. A fifteen-year-old neighbor girl, Dorothy, would cook for us.

Dorothy was pretty with nice skin, light brown hair, and blue eyes. I remember looking at her and wishing I would be pretty like her when I grew up. Since I only had brothers, I enjoyed having a girl in the house while the menfolk worked outside. For a few hours a day it took the sharp edge off of missing Mama so much.

It was a hot summer day. The wood cook stove going full blast in the late afternoon made the kitchen almost unbearable. Days like that, clothes stuck to your back, tempers were short, and you couldn't keep the sweat wiped from your eyes. That's why I played under the shade trees until they called me in for supper.

When I heard the goings-on in the kitchen, I bounded in at full speed. I couldn't believe what I was seeing! Dorothy was trying to cook supper. Grandma was standing between her and the table with her walking stick drawn on her. Dorothy held a bucket of lard in front of her face to ward off the blow. Grandma yelled, "My son works hard to put groceries in this house. No little whippersnapper is going to waste them. You just put that lard down this minute!"

"But—but, I was just going to put a little lard in the biscuits."

"We don't put lard in our biscuits around here. It's too wasteful. I said put it down, girl!"

I stood for a second with my mouth hanging open. I knew Grandma's stick was for walking, but I had never thought of it as a weapon.

Call it luck, fate, whatever. At that instant Volnia appeared and took in the situation. He had been helping Papa and Millard cut logs for our barn raising. He wasted not a second in running for Papa.

Papa stepped into the kitchen and asked, "What's the matter here?"

"She's wasting our lard," Grandma complained, lowering the cane.

"Now, Ma, she's just trying to help us out." As he talked to calm her, he steered her into the front room where she settled in my rocker.

When supper was ready, we all sat at the table and ate. But no one could think of anything interesting to talk about.

Dorothy kept eyeing the back door. She seemed in a big hurry to get the dishes washed and leave for home. Most likely that was a first for her, being threatened with a walking stick.

Millard seemed confused. He came in after the excitement had settled and no one had bothered to explain anything to him.

Volnia looked embarrassed. I happened to know he was sweet on the blue-eyed neighbor. Now Grandma had probably scared her off for good.

Papa looked as if he felt sorry for the girl. But judging from the twinkle in his eye, he must have thought it a little funny.

Grandma looked defeated. She didn't get to be in charge as she had planned. Poor Grandma.

What about me? I just wanted my mama to come home, the sooner the better.

Altha Murphy

THE GHOST STORIES

OO-o-oh! I was scared. I sat up with the others in the front room as long as I dared, or rather, until way past my bedtime. I dreaded going to bed. I was afraid to go into that dark bedroom by myself. But I didn't want anyone to think I was a scaredy cat.

After Grandma came to live with us, she slept in the bed where I had slept in the front room and I slept in the bedroom. That hadn't presented a problem until the night the talk turned to scary things. Even though the door was closed between the two rooms, and I was tucked under the covers, I still heard the conversation. I had to bundle up under the covers, since it was a cold night and there was no heat in that room.

The adults were my parents, my grandma, and two neighbors who had come to visit. My brothers were in there listening, hanging onto every word. The conversation was about ghosts, or haints, as some people called them. According to Grandma, she had seen and heard all kinds of scary things. Doors opened and closed without a cause. Footsteps had gone up and down stairs when everyone was in bed. Sometimes chains had rattled in the middle of the night. Strange lights had traveled a few feet above the ground out in the fields when no one was there. One light had even wandered around in a dark room and suddenly disappeared.

At times Papa said something like "Now, Ma, you know there's no such thing as a haint. If someone looked around, there would be a reasonable explanation for everything."

But that didn't faze Grandma. "Hmmph!" she snorted. "Don't try to tell me that. I reckon I know what I heerd." And on she went.

The visitors helped her out by telling of scary things they had seen and heard. It seemed that a lot of people believed in warnings. If you heard a strange sound and went outside and couldn't find a reason for it, it could be a warning. If so, then very shortly you heard of a death. The noise could sound like beans boiling, someone chopping wood, a chicken sliding on a tin roof, or any number of other things.

I lay shivering under the covers, and not just from the cold. I wondered. Grandma was Papa's mama and she raised him. Surely he must have heard these stories all his life. How come she believed in ghosts and he didn't? Maybe his papa didn't. I wished he had lived long enough for me to know him. Then I could have asked him if a ghost ever got after him.

I scrunched down farther under the covers. I closed my eyes tightly, but sleep didn't come. What was that? Was that a scratch under the window? Did I hear footsteps outside? Oh, no! That couldn't be a chain clanking—or could it? PLOP! The pillow went over my head. Maybe then I couldn't hear the stories from the next room. If any lights floated around, I didn't want to see them. All I wanted was for those people to stop telling those scary stories.

On the other hand, would it be worse when the visitors left? Then everyone would be in bed and there would be nothing but stillness and darkness. I knew for sure it would be dark, but wasn't convinced of the stillness. I whispered under the pillow, "Oh, daylight, please hurry. I need you!"

THE FUNERAL

I wished it could have been a nice warm day. It just didn't seem right to put Grandma into the ground on such a cold blustery day. But it had been two days since she died, and we couldn't keep her out any longer. I don't believe people embalmed their loved ones at that time, at least not in our community.

Grandma was eighty-four and had lived with us four years. She was the only one of my grandparents I knew. The others died before I was born. She was crippled from a childhood disease and walked with a cane. She was so stooped she had to sleep on her sides, never on her back. Her bed was in the front room, along with Papa and Mama's. A wood heater kept the room nice and warm.

Grandma had been sick for a while. When she got really bad, some neighbors came to be with us. In those days it was almost unheard of to go to a hospital, so neighbors came to sit up all night with family members.

The day she died I heard the grownups talk about a death rattle, but I didn't know what that meant. All at once, Grandma sat up in bed. She became straight as an arrow, lay back on her pillow, and stopped breathing. Someone had a hand on her wrist. They said she was gone. I had never seen anyone "go" before. They pulled her eyelids down and put coins on them.

Immediately the family began making arrangements. Millard went to tell our cousins. Papa hitched the team to the wagon and went to see Bro. George McGhehey about conducting the funeral service. Then he went on to Imboden to get Mr. John Jean to make a coffin. Next he stopped by Matthews' store and got some black printed material for a burying dress. It was late when he got home. Some of the neighbors spent the night with us. No family stayed alone when one of their loved ones lay dead.

The next day was busy. Papa went back to town to get the coffin. It was a pine box lined with black satin. A pillow covered with the same material was inside. Mama and the other ladies made the dress. The other women laid Grandma out. That is, they prepared her body for burial. They took down her bed to make room for the coffin and all the people who would come. They couldn't have a fire in that room.

Neighbor men and boys dug the grave with picks and shovels. People didn't have to dig graves for their own loved ones. Others did it out of respect. Sometimes Papa and the boys helped dig graves for other families.

Neighbors stayed again that night. They sat up all night, drinking coffee and talking. I went to bed, but didn't sleep much. After all, my grandma was lying in the next room, cold and stiff in that funny-looking old wood box they called a coffin. I hadn't asked any questions and no one had explained anything. Guess they didn't think I needed to talk about it.

The following day they loaded Grandma into the wagon and we drove a few miles to Friendship Methodist Church. Our family members who had passed on were buried in the cemetery behind the church. It was colder than the day before. After Bro.McGhehey finished the sermon, people stood around talking to my family. I stood off to one side, not knowing what to do. I hadn't cried since it happened and there was a big lump in my throat.

Suddenly I felt an arm across my shoulders. I turned to face a lady who had been at our house the past two days. It was Mrs. Ferrell, who had moved into the community a short while back. She lived there with her children while her husband was away on construction work. She was short, not much taller than I was. She had on a warm furry coat. I buried my face in her shoulder and let the hot tears come. She didn't say a word, just held me while I cried my heart out.

She walked out to the cemetery with me. It's hard to explain, but the lump in my throat was gone. Somehow, I felt a little better. I decided then and there that if I lived to be a hundred, that little lady would always have a special place in my heart.

THE AUNT

I felt sorry for children who didn't have an aunt, especially one like my Aunt Lizzie. I had other aunts at the time, but none who could visit a week or two at a time, like she did.

Her name was really Elizabeth, but I never heard her called that. She was Papa's half sister. She must have been old enough to be his mother, because she had sons about his age. She was a widow and lived with a son and his family. That's why she could visit us any time and stay as long as she wanted.

I loved it when Aunt Lizzie visited. She stayed at the house while Mama helped out in the field. When she wasn't there, I had to go to the field and stay under a tree at the end of the rows while my family worked. I couldn't stay at the house alone. They took an old quilt so I could nap if I got sleepy. Old Jack, our dog, always stayed nearby. It seemed those mornings and afternoons would never end, especially in hot weather when they were chopping cotton. I was always happy when Mama left early to cook the meals, so I could go with her.

Aunt Lizzie paid attention to us kids and we liked that. She cooked and did the rest of the housework. I got to stay with her and was constantly at her heels. She was a good cook and housekeeper. If Mama set a pan of food on the table, she commented, "Gertie, I don't believe I would set the slop pot on the table." Mama thought she was too particular. Papa called it being "nasty nice." But they laughed when they talked about it, so I knew they didn't really mind.

Aunt Lizzie told stories about the family. She told why our forefathers ended up in America. She said my great grandfather or great great grandfather, I can't remember which, was born in Holland. When he was a young lad, probably about fourteen, some people captured him. Shanghaied was the word she used. They forced him to work on a ship headed for America. When they neared New York harbor, he escaped by jumping ship and swimming to shore. As the years passed, he married and had a family. His descendants moved through several states. His Dutch name was hard for the Americans to pronounce, so he shortened it to Milgrim. I know that my grandfather was married at least three times, because there were three sets of children. He finally settled in Arkansas near Imboden at the upper end of Yaeger Hollow.

I was not beyond giving Aunt Lizzie some scares while she watched me. One incident I vaguely remember, but she didn't forget. I was sitting on the front step while she was inside. Suddenly I let out a blood-curdling scream which brought her running. "Child, whatever is the matter?" she yelled as I sat there crying.

A big fat wooly worm was crawling on the step toward me. I pointed to the monster and sobbed, "woo-ey wom." She jerked me up and carried me inside. She couldn't understand why I didn't just get up and move all by myself. I was too scared. I couldn't stand worms then and still can't. That fat ugly thing was coming right at me.

Another scare came when my aunt was peeling apples. I picked up an apple and handed it toward her. "Peel this one next," I said.

She wasn't paying attention and picked up another one instead. Well, I didn't like that one bit. So I ran outside and hid behind a stump. I'd show her! Soon she missed me and began looking. She called and called, but I didn't answer. I could tell by her voice that she was worried. Just let her worry. Let her think maybe I had wandered off to the pond or gone to a neighbor's house. Things became silent and I thought she had gone back inside. I ventured one tiny peek around the stump and she saw me. That ended that little contest. I knew she wouldn't scold me. She never did.

Millard liked her lemon pies. He started asking for them the very day she arrived. That was in a whiny little voice, "I want a lemon pie." Each day he got louder and spread the words out longer. By the third day it was a yell; "I want a lem-m-mon PI-I-IE!" Volnia and I encouraged him to go for it. We knew if he begged long enough and loud enough, lemon pie would turn up on our table.

Aunt Lizzie died when I was young. When I was twelve, Papa found aunt Vert, whose real name was Alverta. She was a full sister to Aunt Lizzie. They had lost contact with each other for thirty-four years. He and I boarded a bus to Wagoner, Oklahoma, to visit her. It was my first trip out of state, my first time on a bus, and the biggest event in my life up to then.

Aunt Vert's daughter, son-in-law, and granddaughter lived next door to her. Roxie, the granddaughter, was close to my age. We shopped in a Piggly Wiggly supermarket, my first. We saw a movie, my second. The title was "Caught in the Draft" and starred Bob Hope.

We swung on a grapevine over a creek. I still have wonderful memories of that trip.

I was happy to meet Aunt Vert, but she looked so much like Aunt Lizzie, I felt a strange longing. When I looked at her, nostalgia washed over me. For some reason I thought about lemon pies.

THE OTHER AUNT

Aunt Lizzie and Aunt Zona were exact opposites in many ways. Aunt Lizzie was tall and thin. Aunt Zona was short and fat. Aunt Lizzie had dark hair, while Aunt Zona's hair was silvery white. Aunt Lizzie was my aunt on Papa's side and Aunt Zona was Mama's sister. Their real names were Elizabeth and Arizona, but no one ever called them that. They were my favorites, although I didn't get to meet some of my aunts, because I came along too late.

When Aunt Lizzie came to visit, she could stay several days. She was a widow and her children were married. When Aunt Zona visited, she had to get back home that day. She had a husband, Uncle George; one daughter, Vera; and four sons; Layton, Sam, Henderson, and Cleo. They lived in the Opposition community about five miles from us.

Once each summer we loaded into the wagon on Saturday and went to visit them, returning on Sunday afternoon. These were the only occasions I recall when my entire family spent the night away from home, except once on an all-night fishing trip.

Naked Ears

I looked forward to those trips for several reasons. For one, they had a store in a big room in their house. I always got candy from the store. They also had a gasoline pump outside. A glass container with big numbers was at the top. Uncle George could tell how many gallons he sold by watching the gas level go down.

They also had a car. Very few times had I been privileged to ride in a car. We went to church with them on Sunday morning. Since there were two girls and six boys, Vera and I rode with the adults and the boys walked. I thought that was a good idea.

A porch went along the front of the house. A swing looked too inviting for me to resist. I spent many hours swinging there, though my feet barely touched the floor.

Something else intrigued me about the house. They had an inside well. A small room enclosed a drilled well. I liked to watch my cousins draw water with the long, tube-like bucket. I couldn't believe they didn't have to go outside to draw water.

Aunt Zona always had a pretty garden the time of year we were there. When families had visitors, the men looked over the crops and livestock. Women looked at the garden, the canned food, the newest quilts, and other handwork. Mama said, "Zona always plants beans on Good Friday, even if it's muddy. She just takes a stick and punches them in the ground." Mama herself wasn't quite that set on a certain day to plant beans.

My favorite room in Aunt Zona's house was the kitchen. A huge blue and white wood cook stove stood at the south end of the long rectangular room. A china closet with curved glass sides graced the other end. In the center sat a table long enough to accommodate a large family. The tantalizing aroma of country ham frying in huge iron skillets was enough to bring a girl from the swing. We drank milk from glasses with stems—goblets, they called them. Milk even tasted better than it did at home.

All the youngsters were older than I, so I didn't play with them when we visited. But I was never bored. No one enjoyed those trips more than I did. The trip to Aunt Zona's was the highlight of the summer, and I looked forward to it from one year to the next.

THE STORIES

I loved the long winter nights. After the work was done, Mama sat by the stand table and read to us by the light of a kerosene lamp.

Millard and Volnia went to Sloan-Hendrix high school in Imboden. Annieville, the school in our community, only went through the eighth grade. Our district had not consolidated with Sloan-Hendrix, so there was no school bus to ride. They got up before daylight to milk eight cows before walking the six miles to school. Besides attending classes, they worked did janitorial work to pay for tuition and books. By the time they walked home and milked the cows again, it was after dark, especially in winter when the days were short.

Papa said he couldn't milk, that he never learned how. That sounded fishy to me, but that's the way it was. He did other chores, like getting in wood and water for the night. He also helped separate the milk after Mama strained it into the big bowl on top of the separator. When he turned the handle, cream came from one spout and skim milk from another.

They shipped the cream to Sugar Creek Creamery in Missouri, so we had a cream check each week. The boys pushed the cans of cream in a wheelbarrow a half mile to the highway. The star route mail carrier picked it up and hauled it to Imboden. From there it went on a train to the creamery.

Everyone was tired after the night chores were done, but then it was study time. At times Mama helped the boys with their English lessons. She only completed the sixth grade and they were in high school. I tried to figure that out. But she knew about nouns and verbs and subjects and objects. She dearly loved to read. We didn't have many books except the Bible, but the boys brought their literature books and library books home.

She read the stories aloud so everyone could listen. Papa went to bed as soon as the chores were done and supper was over. His and Mama's bed was in the front room, so I think he listened to the stories. I know I did. That's how I first heard about Rip Van Winkle, Ichabod Crane, Faust, and lots of others. I didn't understand all the parts, but I stayed awake as long as possible, listening. I usually fell asleep and missed some good parts before being carried to bed.

Education was important in our home. Papa was the oldest of three sons and his father died when they were young. He had to work to help support Grandma and my two uncles. He had little opportunity to attend school, but taught himself a lot. He read the newspapers to keep with the news in Arkansas and in the nation. Voting was a privilege he took seriously even though he had to pay a poll tax to vote. He kept up with the candidates and their platforms so he could decide which ones to support. He was determined his children would get an education, no matter what.

My grade school didn't have a library, but the readers were filled with good stories. Young children not only read stories in their readers, but they also listened as the older ones read their stories and did their recitations.

I was six when my brothers entered high school. They graduated before I started. But I always looked forward to the time when I would have a library full of books at my fingertips. When my time came, I lived with Mrs. Miller in town and helped her for my room and board. She was a cultured little southern lady who nurtured my love of reading. I also learned social skills from her.

I have never stopped reading, but no story has characters or plot more intriguing than those I heard at my mother's knee so many years ago. It would be hard to read by a kerosene lamp now and keep a drafty room warm with a wood stove. But we didn't miss what we had never had.

Naked Ears

THE HOG KILLING

"The Hog Killing" Men working on two hogs hanging from tree. Note scalding barrel in foreground.

Hog killing took place on one of the coldest days of winter. It had to be that way, since the meat might spoil on a warmer day. We usually killed two hogs to provide our meat for the winter, except for an occasional chicken or squirrel.

Two hogs had been fattening in a pen below the barn for a few weeks. Now that they were fat enough and the weather was cold, it was time to butcher them. Butchering hogs was a big job, usually too much for one family. Neighbor men were there to help. Papa shot the hogs in the head and the other men slit their throats immediately so they would bleed properly.

My brothers drew water from the cistern and heated it in a big barrel outside. The men sloshed the hogs, one at a time up and down in the scalding water to loosen the hair. They hung them from a tree and removed the hair by scraping the skin with sharp knives. The next step was splitting them down the middle to take out the insides. Then it was time to cut them into pieces.

By that time it was almost noon. That first meal consisted of fresh liver and tenderloin, along with Mama's fluffy biscuits and gravy. My mouth had been watering for that meal since they first started the process. The neighbor men ate with us, and they also took some fresh meat home. When my folks helped other families kill hogs, they always brought meat home.

That afternoon it was time to begin working up the meat. They trimmed the fat and laid it aside. Papa had a big meat box in the smokehouse where he salted down the hams, shoulders, and jowls. Next came the sausage making. They put strips of lean meat and fat through the sausage mill. Seasoning it just right was an art. I enjoyed turning the handle on the sausage mill. That was my contribution.

We used parts of the meat fresh, like tenderloin, liver, ribs, and some of the sausage. Mama liked souse, or head cheese, and she used the head for that. She even cooked the feet and thought they were good. Ugh! I never tasted them, but declared I didn't like them.

The work could not be completed in one day. Neighbor women came the second day to help. What sausage we didn't eat fresh was fried and canned. Mama used the extra fat to render into lard. She did this outside in the iron wash kettle. She made cracklings from the skin. That's why we sometimes had crackling cornbread.

After the fresh meat was gone, I didn't eat anything but lean meat from the hams and shoulders and sausage. I suppose the youngest child in every family hears, "You let her get by with things we didn't."

My brothers said I was spoiled. They said they always had to eat the fat along with the lean, but I was allowed to leave the fat on my plate. Parents probably do mellow by the time the third child comes along. Oh, well, I was the baby of the family and the only girl. Anyway, my cats were happy that I didn't like fat meat.

THE BARN RAISING

A barn raising was a special occasion. We had lots of company the day we had ours, because families came from all around to help.

Papa and the boys had worked like crazy to get enough logs ready. They cut trees, trimmed the branches off, and dragged them from the woods. They cut the logs the right length for the walls and stacked them near where the barn would stand.

Papa had also been busy making shingles. He was good at that and I loved to watch him work. He took a block of wood and placed it on a larger block, which he called the chopping block. He put a froe on the top block and hammered it in. The wood sliced off into thin pieces called shingles. They would be used for the barn roof.

Neighbor men and older boys helped notch the ends of the logs and lift them into place. Gradually the walls went up, log by log.

Men and boys were not the only ones involved on barn raising day. They could work up enormous appetites with all that notching and lifting. That's where the ladies and older girls fit in. Their task was to have the table filled with food at noon.

Mama had planned for days. The day before the barn raising she baked pies and a cake. That morning before the neighbors arrived, she had Papa kill two chickens which she fried to a golden brown. She gathered fresh vegetables from the garden.

The other ladies also brought food. They came along in the wagons with their husbands and children. They, along with Mama, worked all morning in the kitchen preparing the delicious meal.

At noon the workers came in and we all enjoyed a feast. One lady commented,"It took us hours to get this meal together, and just a few minutes for it to disappear." We had three meals each day — breakfast, dinner, and supper. I don't believe I had heard the noon meal referred to as lunch at that time.

After dinner the men relaxed in the shade a while before returning to work. Before the women relaxed, they pitched in to wash the dishes. Then they had the entire afternoon to visit. Not that they hadn't talked already, but now they could do it in a more leisurely fashion. When the children stopped playing for a few minutes to rest, they might hear talk of who had been sick, or who had a new baby, or who had just married. In case of the latter, there would be plans in the making for a charivari (shiv o ree). Or they might hear about canning, gardening, sewing, new recipes, or remedies for sickness.

In my opinion, we children profited most from the whole operation. We played all morning, stuffed ourselves at noon, and played all afternoon.

By the end of the day, the walls of a new barn stood between the house and the pond. They didn't get the roof on that day. Papa and the boys would do that the next few days. The barn would be a source of pride for many years to come. There was a loft for hay. The roof would extend on each side to provide shelter from harsh weather.

It was a day of hard work, but also one of pleasure. It was an opportunity for people to enjoy a social gathering. Millard liked the joke about the three best means of communication — telegraph, telephone, and tell a woman. We didn't have telegraph, we didn't have telephones, but news got around in our neighborhood. Some reasons for that may have been occasions like barn raisings, hog killings, quilting parties, church gatherings with dinner on the ground, school programs, and charavaris.

Altha Murphy

During the decade of the 30s no one had money to hire workers. But when a family needed something done, neighbors responded. That's one reason people in the Annieville community survived the Great Depression.

THE SORGHUM MILL

It wasn't any fun getting cane ready to take to the sorghum mill. We could tell when it was ready to cut by the way the heads on the stalks looked.

When I was younger, I didn't have anything to do with the cane, other than breaking off some joints to peel and chew to get that sweet juice out. But the time came when I was big enough to get in on the action. I couldn't cut and top it, because I didn't need to handle the knives, but I helped strip the leaves off.

The sun beat down unmercifully in the cane patch. The tall stalks didn't allow a breeze to come through. At times I felt I would indeed croak, but I never did.

When the stalks were cut, topped, and stripped, it was time to stack them neatly in the wagon. Then away we went to Mr. Buster Lawrence's sorghum mill about a mile away. I wouldn't have missed that trip for the world.

Sorghum making was something to see. A horse or mule was hitched to a machine and went around in a circle. That caused two big rollers to turn, squeezing the juice from the cane stalks. Someone stood and fed the stalks into the rollers. The juice went into a metal pan with seven sections, cooking all along the way. By the time it was ready to take from the last section, it was finished. What went in as green juice came out as thickened light amber colored molasses.

From the last pan, Mr. Lawrence let the sorghum out into shiny new gallon buckets and put lids on them. He said, "Three for him, one for me." As he said this, he placed three buckets in one spot and one in another. That meant he kept one bucket in four for his work. It was a good deal for him and for us. We couldn't make our own because we didn't have a mill. We probably wouldn't have known how, anyway, for there seemed to be an art to it. He could keep what his family needed and sell the rest.

Mr. Lawrence could not have run this operation alone. His wife and children worked as hard as he did. Each one knew what to do and just when to do it. When I saw them working over that hot pan, I decided stripping cane wasn't the hottest job in the world.

Kids found interesting things to do at the mill besides watching the sorghum made. A big pummy pile was always nearby. Pummy was what was left of the stalks after the juice had been squeezed out.

We played on the pile and slid down it. Foam formed on the sorghum while it cooked and was skimmed off. We could get a joint of cane and dip into the foam. It tasted good that way, but it was better if we held it over the chimney at the end of the pan and let it toast.

When we left home, our wagon was loaded with green stalks of cane. When we returned, we had several shiny buckets of new molasses, enough to last until the next fall, if we were lucky.

We used most of the sorghum stirred with butter and eaten on hot biscuits. It was good to put in cakes and cookies. It was also good for peanut brittle and taffy. But my favorite way to eat it was in big fluffy popcorn balls. Nothing tasted better on a cold winter night.

Altha Murphy

THE REMEDIES

The best thing a child growing up during the Great Depression could do was stay healthy. There were no telephones in our community and the nearest doctors were six miles away. On those rare occasions when an illness or accident was serious enough to require a doctor, someone had to go to town by wagon or horseback to get one. As a result, each family had remedies for almost all sorts of ailments.

We didn't have many fresh fruits and vegetables through the winter. So when springtime came it was time for a tonic to build good blood. Sassafras tea was one remedy for that. Another was sulfur mixed with sorghum molasses. The tea wasn't bad, but the sulfur ruined the taste of the sorghum.

Baking soda in water was good for heartburn and upset stomach, or so Papa said. I didn't have to take that because I didn't have heartburn in those days.

Cloverine salve seemed to be good for sores, scratches, and scrapes. Periodically someone came around selling it. We always kept the salve on hand.

Quinine was good for malaria. It came in a dark blue bottle. A dose was what one could hold on the end of a knife blade.

A wad of wet chewing tobacco could take the edge off stings from wasps, bees, and hornets. Prince Albert was a substitute if no one around chewed tobacco. One hot summer day Millard and I went to Yaeger Hollow with some other young people. I can't remember why we went. What stands out in my memory is that a hornet stung me near the eye. Within minutes my whole face was swollen and did it ever hurt! We walked a mile out of our way to Mr. and Mrs. Hall's house because we knew he chewed tobacco. Mrs. Hall fixed me up and the next day it was better, although I still had a honey of a shiner.

Epsom salts dissolved in hot water was used for swelling. It also helped to prevent blood poisoning after an insect bite or a small wound.

At the first sign of a sore throat, one gargled with hot salt water. That was repeated as often as necessary.

Almost everyone had a different remedy for poison ivy and poison oak. Different ones recommended baking soda and water paste, soda and buttermilk, and a soda and vinegar mixture.

Watkins liniment was an old standby for my parents. A peddler came by selling it and we were never out of it. He also sold other items, especially flavoring. The liniment was rubbed on for all kinds of aches and pains.

When I got a cold, I got Vicks salve rubbed on my chest. It was hard to sleep smelling that all night. Some of my friends had to take a few drops of turpentine in a spoonful of sugar for colds.

Babies were not left out. If one had the colic, he got a few drops of paragoric. It could be bought at the drugstore without a prescription. If a baby was trying to break out in hives and couldn't, women knew just what to do. They baked an onion and fed him the juice. Next thing you knew, that baby was as spotted as a speckled pup. Then he seemed to feel better.

First, second, and third runners-up for bad were the laxatives, Black Draught, castor oil, and senna leaf tea. I never took Black Draught, but heard how terrible it was from my friends. Once that castor oil got in your mouth, it slid right down. But it did taste awful. Only once did I resist taking it. After I got my nose held so I had to swallow it, I wished I had been more cooperative. As for the senna tea, I wished Mama had forgotten where those old plants grew. They were behind the chicken house and I suspected she had planted them there.

The prizewinner for bad was the remedy for croup. When I had croup, Mama cooked chopped-up onions. She sewed them in a little cloth bag, a poultice, she called it. She slapped that thing on my chest, covered me up tightly, and expected me to sleep. Have you ever tried to sleep with a bag of hot onions right under your nose?

All those remedies were meant to help after you became ill. Steps were also taken to keep us from getting sick. They were shots and vaccinations.

The county health nurse came to school on a regular basis and set up shop. She had a burner under a pan where she boiled needles. We lined up and, one by one, stuck out our arms for typhoid shots. The longer we stood in line, the bigger those needles looked and the more we dreaded it. Some kids in the line ahead hollered and carried on when they got their shots. Hearing them didn't help a bit. When my turn came, I didn't dare look.

For the smallpox vaccination, the nurse rubbed medicine on the arm. She jabbed a needle in several times to punch the medicine in. I got so sick after my vaccination I missed a week of school. But after it healed, I had a beauty of a scar to show for the ordeal.

If one set of parents didn't know the remedy for a certain illness, you could be sure someone would tell them. People said the remedy was much better than the ailment. At times I wondered.

THE CREEPY CRAWLIES

Why would anyone think of selling a bug? Even more puzzling was why anyone would want to buy one. Yet, that's what went on day after day, week after week, in our neighborhood.

Boys of all sizes raked in ponds, looked under logs and leaves, and caught everything that crawled, hopped, or flew. They took them to Mr. Byron Marshall and he bought whatever they had. His motto seemed to be, "You catch it—I'll buy it." That gave the boys a little spending money. It also allowed them to scare girls with the creepy crawlies.

Mr. Marshall collected those creatures for a reason. When asked about his reason, he explained, "I supply colleges and universities across the country with different specimens. I exchange with other collectors, and eventually I hope to have a museum and charge a fee to go through it.

He added, "I used to have a lot more than I do now, but a fire destroyed my home and I lost everything. Now I am trying to replace what I lost."

Mr. Marshall lived on a farm a mile north of us if we went straight through the woods, "as the crow flies." It was farther if we went the long way around. He lived with his mother who was a widow. They rented ground to us because he didn't want to farm it and we needed more land to grow what we needed.

Their rooms were filled with all kinds of butterflies, bugs, spiders, frogs, snakes, lizards, lampreys, dragonflies, praying mantises, salamanders, worms, ticks, fleas, wasps, hornets, bees, snakes, and anything else one could imagine. That man seemed to know everything there was to know about biology.

Butterflies and insects were framed under glass. I felt sorry for them as they hung with pins stuck through them. Labels told what kind they were and whether they were male or female. Other creatures were pickled in alcohol. There they sat on shelves in jars of all sizes with labels neatly attached. Several animals were stuffed, but he kept most of them in other places.

My brothers spent their spare time catching whatever they ran across. They didn't catch poisonous snakes, but our cousin Eli did. He put a forked stick down behind their heads, then picked them up in the same place so they couldn't bite him, and put them in containers.

I liked to go to the Marshalls' house when my folks went to work in their fields. But I didn't go to see the creepy crawlies. I played under a nice shade tree in their yard. Once a week Mrs. Marshall baked yeast bread. She wrapped the loaves in clean white cloths and stored them in a lard stand. That lasted them until the next baking day. I always got some buttered slices when she took the loaves from the oven. So I tried to plan my visits to coincide with baking days.

While I was there, I looked at the butterflies and some of the insects. As for the rest, I tried to avoid them. Ugh!

It seemed strange that people bought and sold creepy crawlies. It seemed even stranger that anyone would ever pay to see them. But that's exactly what happened. After a few years, Mr. Marshall moved his collection to Imboden and opened his museum. I went on a field trip to the museum when I was in high school. Several years after that, he opened a museum in the Hot Springs area. From all reports, he had a successful business there.

Of course, I didn't get to visit on bread baking days after the Marshalls left our community. But I still have delightful memories of the aroma from that oven and the taste of that fresh bread loaded down with butter.

THE FISH TRAP

The fish trap sounded like a great idea. Since my brothers didn't have a lot of time to fish, and since we all liked to eat fish, they came up with a plan. They found a hollow log and boarded up one end of it. Then they waded out into the middle of the pond and laid the log on the bottom. "You see," Volnia explained, "the fish will swim in at the open end of the log. Once they get in there, they won't be able to turn around or back out, so they will be trapped."

The boys normally didn't care about me following around after them, but the next day after they laid the trap, I had a special invitation to go the pond with them.

"Why?" I wanted to know.

"We need you," Millard said. "You can help us."

"How can I help you?" I was a bit suspicious. Surely they didn't expect me to wade out in that pond and get all wet and muddy.

"You can grab the fish when we dump them on the bank."

I hesitated. Standing on the bank and catching the fish wouldn't be so bad.

"Do you want fish for supper, or don't you?" he demanded.

That convinced me. I trailed after them. They placed a big bucket of water by me and told me to wait. They waded into the pond and took hold of the log. It was much heavier than when they put it in. Not only was it filled with water, but it was also waterlogged. They heaved and tugged and pulled and pushed until they finally got the end of the log on the bank. The rest would be a piece of cake. Now all they had to do was lift the other end of the log and let me grab the fish.

So there I stood, my feet far apart, my hands on my knees, waiting. I could almost taste that crispy brown fish now. I hoped it would be a whopper.

Splash! There it came at last. But wait a minute. What was that wiggling and squirming at my feet? It wasn't a fish at all. It was a nasty, slimy, crawly old snake!

I let out a scream and headed for the house. I wasn't running. I was leaping and bounding. Each time my feet hit the ground, I let out another whoop.

Mama came running to the back porch to see what was going on. She just knew something terrible had happened with all that screeching. I tried to stop long enough to tattle on them, but my breath was almost gone. "Th-th-they tried to m-m-make me catch an old sn-sn-snake!"

By that time the boys were on their way to the house, explaining as they came. They declared they didn't do it on purpose. How could they know a snake would be in the log?

They finally got me calmed down enough to listen. They did look pitiful, standing there with their overall legs rolled up and mud up to their knees, both talking at once. I glared at them, but couldn't help halfway believing them. After all, they were hoping for a fish supper just as much as I was.

I still wished a big fish had been caught in the trap. It would have tasted much better than that old fat back we had almost every night. At least, the others had it almost every night. I didn't eat it.

I had an important announcement for them. "From now on, you're on your own with your fishing. If you catch fish with or without a trap, don't expect any help from me."

Altha Murphy

THE CISTERN

I awoke and rubbed my eyes. Why was I feeling so good when I went to sleep? Then I remembered. Soon we wouldn't have to carry water any longer. We were getting a new cistern and would be able to step right off the back porch and draw all the water we needed.

All my life we had carried water for drinking, cooking, bathing, and washing clothes. Millard and Volnia used the wheelbarrow to push ten-gallon cream cans filled with water. Sometimes they carried it in ten-quart buckets. When I went along, I could use a small lard bucket.

We got water from Lloyd and Myrtle Reed's well when we could. It was a drilled well. It was just a round hole in the ground with metal casing. The bucket was a long tube-like object which just fit into the hole. It was tied to a rope which went through a pulley. The water was cold when it was first drawn.

If that well got low, we had to get water from the Evergreen well three quarters of a mile away. That was different; it was a dug well. It was much larger across and had rocks cemented together around the top. People tied a rope to their own water bucket and let it down to fill

Naked Ears

with water. That well never went dry. Folks all around talked about how cold and good the Evergreen well water was.

In the summer it was hot going barefoot on the dirt road. The dust was deep and so hot it burned my feet. At times I stubbed my toes or got a stone bruise on my heel.

Often Papa and they boys hitched the team and put barrels in the wagon. They went to a spring about three miles away to get water. I liked to go with them and enjoy the ride through the woods.

Sometimes my family hauled water for washing clothes. At other times we went to Cooper's Creek to wash. That was a fun day for me, a workday for the others. They loaded up the iron wash kettle, tubs, washboard, lye soap, and food for dinner. They built a fire under the kettle to heat water. Some clothes dried on bushes while the others were being washed and while we ate. Others were taken home to be dried on clotheslines. Washing took almost all day, so everyone was tired when we got home.

We were excited about the cistern at the southeast corner of the house. Papa and another man dig a big, deep round hole. I wondered what they were doing when I saw them let a lighted lantern down into the hole. "Why did you put the lantern down?" I asked Papa.

"If the lantern stays lit, we'll know it's safe for us to work down there," he said.

The man cemented the big hole all around. They built a wood frame with a cover at the top. They placed wood troughs all around the edges of the roof so rain water could run into the cistern.

My parents said we could only catch water in the cistern during months with the letter r in their names. That left out May, June, July, and August. I didn't understand what the letter r had to do with water in our cistern.

"Why can't we catch water all year?" I asked.

"Because the months left out are summer months," Mama said. "We might get wigglers in the water then and they would ruin it." Wigglers were baby mosquitoes.

Some people put butter and milk in a bucket and let it down into their wells and cisterns to keep cool. Papa wouldn't allow us to do that. "What if we spilled milk in the water. Wouldn't we be in a fix then?" he said.

As soon as we caught enough water to use, we could stop carrying it and hauling it. And, oh yes, there was a bonus. A huge mound of dirt was now in our back yard. I knew that as soon as the Bermuda grass covered it, I could run up and down on my own private mountain. That's why I had gone to bed happy and awoke with something to look forward to.

THE RADIO

Life in the Annieville community saw a dramatic change when the radio was introduced. After that, everyone had something to do on Saturday nights. People were tired from working in the fields and doing housework all week and needed a break from the routine.

At first only a few families owned a radio. Now on Saturdays after we milked the cows, fed the chickens, and did the supper dishes, my family sometimes walked to a neighbor's house to listen to the Grand Ole Opry. We were amazed that the program came all the way from Nashville, Tennessee, and we could hear it right there in their front room. It came on at eight o'clock and lasted until midnight.

At times only my brothers went to the neighbor's house. They didn't want to leave before the program was over and I always got sleepy when it got late. Then I didn't want to walk home and I was too heavy to carry.

On that particular night, it didn't matter if I did get sleepy and doze off. We had our own radio! It was funny-looking, but it played just fine. We bought it from a man who took it out of a car. It was hooked up to a car battery, but who cared? We listened to it each day, especially the news and music programs. We had to be careful to not use it too much, so the battery would last as long as possible.

That night we were expecting several people to visit us and listen to the Grand Ole Opry. News had spread that we had a radio. Some would come who had radios of their own, because it was the in thing to make the occasion into a social gathering. At exactly eight o'clock, George D. Hay, the Solemn Old Judge, would yell, "Let 'er go, boys, let 'er go!" Then the music began. I liked to hear Uncle Dave Mason play and sing, because I learned that October 12 was his birthday, the same as mine.

I knew the routine. After a few songs, a man came on and told what good biscuits you could make using Martha White flour. Then Minnie Pearl came on with her "How-dee-ee-ee!" I'm just so glad to be here. I'm just so glad I could come!" She told about the crazy things her Uncle Nabob and Brother had done that week. I thought she must have a strange family. I felt sorry for her, too. It seemed that no matter how hard she tried, she just couldn't manage to find a boy friend. It wasn't because she was bashful, I decided, because she certainly talked enough.

Altha Murphy

I couldn't wait for sundown to come. I was anxious to do my part to get ready. Mama said, "After you get through with the dishes, you can take care of the lamps."

That meant filling the kerosene lamps, trimming their wicks, and cleaning their chimneys. Dirty chimneys didn't let much light shine through. I knew how to clean them. I took wadded-up newspapers and rubbed the inside to get the black off. Then I washed them in warm soapy water, rinsed them, and let them dry. I secretly wished we had an Aladdin lamp like some of my friends did. I had never seen anything put out so much light. Maybe someday, I thought, as I cleaned and dreamed.

The front room would be crowded. People would sit in the rockers and on the bed. We would bring in straight chairs from the kitchen. Some might even sit on the porch, since it was summer and the doors were open.

The preacher might see some sleepy people in church Sunday morning. But we wouldn't worry about that on this special Saturday night. We were more than ready to welcome Judge Hay, Uncle Dave, Minnie Pearl, and all the others into our home.

THE PETTICOAT

Things sounded pretty exciting in the kitchen when I awoke that morning. I wanted to hurry to see what was going one. But first I had to get dressed. You didn't go into the front room before you were completely dressed. Oh, you could put shoes and stockings on sitting by the heater when it was cold. But on this day I wasn't wearing shoes. It was summer.

I was not allowed to go around the house in a gown or petticoat. That wasn't decent. I had heard that some people had housecoats to wear over their gowns, but I had never owned one.

After getting dressed in record time, I rushed to the kitchen. I couldn't believe my eyes! There stood Mama at the table, making biscuits, wearing only her petticoat and waist. She didn't call it a blouse—it was her waist.

Papa was there, too. Thus the loud talking. "Woman, what is the meaning of this? Have you taken leave of your senses? Don't you know the boys will be in any minute? No one cooks breakfast looking like that!"

Papa always got up first and built a fire in the wood cook stove. Then he jumped back into bed. When the fire got hot, Mama got up and cooked. Then the rest of us got up to eat. Papa was probably asleep when she got up that morning.

Mama said, "I've been telling you for some time I needed some material. I wore those two old black skirts as long as I could. They were so worn I couldn't patch the patches. So I stuck them in the stove when I got up." While she talked she kept on cooking, just like it was the most normal thing in the world to cook breakfast in one's petticoat.

"You what?" thundered Papa.

"That's right. They've already gone up in smoke."

It's not as if it were not a pretty petticoat. Mama had made it from white sacks and crocheted lace all around the bottom. It was starched and ironed all nice and smooth. I happened to know it had lace at the top, too, as well as some embroidered flowers. But that part was hidden from view beneath her waist. Even if the top had been visible, Papa wouldn't have been impressed.

"But why didn't you tell me?" he demanded.

"I did, several times," she answered matter-of-factly. "You always had so many other things on your mind you didn't seem to pay attention."

Papa scratched his head and stroked his chin. His bright blue eyes looked troubled, like he was thinking important thoughts. Now the only sounds in the kitchen were bacon and eggs frying and the oven door closing as Mama checked on the biscuits.

When Millard and Volnia came in for breakfast, Papa announced they would be cutting sprouts in the new ground that day. "Cutting sprouts?" Volnia echoed. "You said we would lay the corn by today. It's too hot to cut sprouts."

"Yeah," Millard chimed in. "It's a lot easier to plow between the corn rows for the last time. It's hard work to stoop over and cut sprouts all over that new ground. That axe gets hard to handle. Anyway, the sprouts just come back and we'll have to do it all over again. I'd rather lay the corn by, like you said last night."

"I know what I said, but plans have changed," Papa said. I need the team today. I'll hitch them while you boys milk. I'm going to town."

"You? To Town? Today?" Volnia repeated. Boy, I thought, he's getting really good at that echoing business. The boys were so dumbfounded by this information they hadn't seemed to notice that Mama was not quite up to snuff in her appearance.

Things were unusually quite during breakfast. No one seemed to have anything worthwhile to say.

Soon Papa was on his way. Under other circumstances, I would have been at his heels. But everything happened so fast, I didn't even ask this time. Anyway, he didn't seem to be in a very good mood.

After he left, I asked Mama, "Why did he leave in such a hurry?"

"I'm not sure," she answered. "But if I had to guess, I'd say he will head straight for Matthews' store and ask to see their yard goods."

When Papa returned that afternoon, he had two pieces of material, a brown print and a black one. Mama didn't say much, but I could have sworn I saw her smile to herself.

The old treadle sewing machine hummed the next two days. Mama had not one dress, but two. Never again was she caught cooking breakfast in her petticoat, even if it did have pretty lace on the bottom.

THE ORCHARD

Too bad everyone didn't have an orchard. We had five acres of apple trees and lots of things could happen there.

Apples were a money crop for us. The trees required a lot of work. Five times a year, Papa sprayed them. He mixed different powders and crystals with water and put them in a barrel with a pump and a nozzle. He hauled the barrel in a wagon from tree to tree. Someone had to drive the team and pump while he sprayed the trees. He knew just what kind of spray the trees needed at different times of the year.

At times the trees needed pruning. One year Papa hired Mr. Haney, a neighbor, to prune them. When I came home from school and saw how the limbs had been lopped off, I said, "What happened? Our trees are ruined. We won't ever have apples again."

"You'll see," said Papa. They will bloom out next spring prettier than ever."

He was right. They had pink blossoms galore in the spring and more apples than usual in the fall.

In early fall, all that work paid off. We had a few June apple trees, but those were mainly for our own use. In the fall, branches loaded with red and yellow delicious apples. Papa put an ad in *The Imboden Journal*, that the apples would be ready on a certain day.

When that day arrived, we got up before daylight to get the chores done. By sunup, people began coming from town and all around the countryside. They came all day long, bringing baskets, buckets, boxes, and tow sacks. Some let us shake the trees and pick the apples off the ground. Others didn't want their apples bruised, so we hand-picked those. Papa always rounded the baskets up, saying he was giving them good old Methodist measure.

Apple day was exciting for us. We saw lots of people and heard the latest news. By nightfall, we were dead tired. Papa grinned and said he had to walk sideways because of so much money in his overall pockets. No wonder! He got fifty cents for each bushel we sold. Most of the apples were sold that day, but not all. A few people came later and we peddled the rest.

One year we had a good laugh on Papa. He peddled apples at the tri-county fair in Imboden. A Gypsy fortune teller tried to barter with him, his fortune for a peck of apples. When he told her no deal, she said she would buy a peck. He handed her the apples and she went into the tent to get his money, or so she said. He waited and waited, but she didn't come back out. He took a lot of kidding about raising apples for the Gypsies.

Besides growing apples to sell, we had all we could use. We had fried apples all summer and fall. We had applesauce, pies, jelly, and preserves all year. We wrapped some to keep into the winter. We had one tree of Winesaps and they were better for keeping.

Those were the reasons we had the orchard. But I liked it for other reasons. It was a great place to go when I was mad after a switching or a scolding. When that happened, I took Old Jack, our dog, and sat under a tree behind the barn. I didn't want anyone to know where I was. Let them think I had disappeared, it would serve them right. I might cry, or I might tell Old Jack how mean everyone was to me. He stretched out on the ground with his head on his paws and listened to every word. Sometimes he wagged his tail to let me know he thought they were mean, too. That helped.

I also went to the orchard for fun. It was a great place to take my friends to climb trees and eat green apples. Mama said, "I declare, I believe that girl starts eating green apples as soon as they shed the blooms."

She warned me I might get a stomachache. They were so good, I figured if I did get a stomachache, it would be worth it.

The orchard was a wonderful place for dreaming. I could sit on the grass under a tree and think about life. I could dream all I wanted, and it didn't cost a penny. I thought about how I would grow up and get married, and have a family all my own. I would have a big house with a yard full of beautiful flowers. My husband would be the most handsome man around. I would have at least two little girls, so each would have a sister to play with, something I never had. I kept telling Mama I wanted one, but it didn't do any good.

One afternoon I was up in a tree because I was sad. We had a white chicken named Crip. I named him that because he was crippled in one leg. Since he was frying sized, Mama asked me if she could fry him for dinner. I told her it was okay, but later I climbed the tree and cried. It was the first time I ever turned down fried chicken, biscuits, and gravy. I wasn't hungry.

Altha Murphy

THE PICTURE

Marian Chambers (left) and Altha on Marian's 10th birthday.

It was all I could do to put one foot in front of the other. Not only was I dead tired, but a cloud of dread hovered above. I was supposed to be home by five o'clock and it was almost six. More than likely, Mama would take a peach tree switch to my legs. Peach tree tea, she called it.

Papa didn't switch me, but he talked. Oh, boy, could he ever talk when I had done something wrong. I would have chosen a dose of peach tree tea any day over one of his talks. How was I to know when I left that morning the day would turn out like it did?

They had let me walk about a mile to my friend Marian's house to play all day. But they warned that I must be home by five o'clock. Marian lived across and down from the country store, but I didn't stop there. I had no pennies for candy or gum that day.

Marian was excited when I arrived at her house. That was her tenth birthday. I was only seven, but we were good friends. There were few playmates nearby. She wanted to do something special, so her mother told her we could walk the five miles into Imboden. Her grandfather was a photographer there and he would take our picture.

He lived with a daughter and her family. I remembered him because he had taken a picture of my family once.

Her mother said we could eat dinner there, then walk back home. That sounded like a super idea to me. Suddenly an ordinary day was turning into an adventure.

It was fun going to town. It was such a grownup thing to do. We went past a pine grove and made it down the "Big Hill" just fine. When we came to the cedar glade, we had to stop and rest on a rock.

When we arrived the grandfather was happy to see us. He took us into a room and stood us before a picture-taking machine. It had a cloth over it and he put his head under the cloth. One big flash, and it was all over. We ate a good dinner and had a nice visit.

The sun was getting over in the western sky when we decided to head for home. Where had the day gone? The way back seemed much farther. That morning we had come down the big hill, but now we had to climb it. We stopped to rest more often than we did coming down. It was tiring, but we didn't mind because we had enjoyed the day. We talked about the picture and wondered how it would turn out.

It wasn't until we got back to Marian's house that I began to worry. Their clock showed a quarter to six and I hit out for home. As I trudged along, I wished there were some way to avoid facing the music for being an hour late.

I went through the front gate and saw my parents on the front porch. They looked worried. They wanted to know why I was late and I spilled the entire story. They couldn't believe it. They were more upset because we had walked to town by ourselves than because I was an hour late. I could almost feel that switch wrapping around my bare legs. I would be so glad to get this night over.

Then I began listening to the conversation. "She's not the one to blame. That woman should have known better than to let two little girls walk ten miles alone," Mama said. It had been twelve for me, but I didn't remind them of that little detail. The situation was looking brighter by the minute.

There was no punishment. Honestly, I think they were glad I was home safe and sound.

My feet and legs were aching and tomorrow I would be sore all over. But that was a small price to pay for such a wonderful time on a lovely summer day. The best part was yet to come. In a few days we would have pictures of our very own to keep. I couldn't wait to see them.

THE SOUTHERN LADIES

When someone is described as a little old southern lady, a picture immediately forms in my mind. No doubt this is because I had contact with a couple of those in my early childhood.

Before I was born, my family lived back in the woods a few miles from state highways and county roads. Only wagon lanes led to houses in the upper portion of Yaeger Hollow, or Yaeger Holler, as it was commonly called. The original house was built of logs, but rooms had been added over the years. My papa, the oldest of three sons, was the last to marry, so he lived on the home place with his mother after his father died and his brothers married. After my parents married, they continued to live there and my brothers were born there.

When Millard was seven and Volnia was four, it was time to make a big decision. They needed to move closer to a school. Millard hadn't been to school yet, since he would have had to walk alone four miles through the woods to Oak Leaf School. So they sold the home place and bought forty acres in the flatwoods, a mile from Annieville School. The boys started together in the first grade. By the time I was born, the family had built and settled into a four room house.

Mr. and Mrs. William Hall came from Memphis and bought the home place in the woods. A farmer he was not. He had lived in the city, collecting debts for companies, for many years. So he and Papa struck a deal with benefits for both. Papa would raise the crops and they would share the yield.

Enter the southern ladies. When Mr. Hall came to Lawrence County, he brought his wife Sally with him. Much of the time her sister, Miss Ethel Hargrove, lived with them. Those two ladies had a proper upbringing in Mississippi and had lived in Memphis several years.

I thought the two ladies' talk sounded a little strange. The end of words ending in er was pronounced with an a. They talked about their fatha and their motha, and even about how good pot licka was. That was a new one on me, or as Mama would say, a new wrinkle on my horn. Imagine my surprise when I learned they were merely talking about liquid left in the iron pots after cooking greens or beans. We had never called it pot liquor, just bean soup or greens soup.

At any rate, I liked to hear them talk about their life in Mississippi as children and young girls. I also liked to spend time at their house.

Naked Ears

Often I went with my folks when they worked in the fields. I could spend a night or two and go home whenever they decided I should. It was about two miles between our houses if we went straight through the woods.

A creek babbled at the foot of the hill below their house. I could go there to wade or just sit and daydream. I could pick wild flowers and make necklaces or garlands. At night we heard animals in the woods, especially owls.

It was a treat to eat at Mrs. Hall's table. When she made biscuits, she rolled the dough thin and folded it back over itself. She used a biscuit cutter and I noticed how tiny they looked compared to Mama's big ones. After they baked, it was easy to pull them apart and load them down with real country butter. When the butter melted, we turned the buttered sides up and doused them with Log Cabin syrup. The syrup container was metal and looked like a log cabin. The place on top where the syrup came out looked like the chimney. For some reason, biscuits and syrup are not nearly as tasty as they were in those days.

Like other families, the Halls raised chickens for eggs and meat. Those southern ladies knew how to fry chicken to perfection.

However, one day when everyone had a hankering for chicken, things didn't turn out so well. Mr. Hall tried to shoot a fryer. Suddenly his wife yelled, "Bill Hall, you shot me!" The bullet had missed the chicken and grazed her leg. It wasn't a bad wound, but that provided enough excitement for one day.

Mrs. Hall had beautiful dishes which I admired. I was fond of a cut glass dinner bell. She said it would be mine after she was through with it. I didn't get the bell, but I did get a cut glass cake plate which was bought in 1895, Mama's birth year. Years later, when my husband, Truett, and I were in college in Arkadelphia, we lived in a mobile home. I stored the plate under the refrigerator. When we sold the trailer and moved into a house, the plate was forgotten. I didn't think of it for some time, so it is long gone.

Therefore, I don't have any mementos of the southern ladies, just memories. It was probably the first contact I had with people whose culture was a wee bit different from ours, but knowing them was a pleasant experience.

THE APRON

The apron, like many other objects of yesteryear, has faded into the nostalgic past. But it once held a place of prominence, even of necessity, in the home. No mother or grandmother was properly dressed in the morning without one.

There were two kinds, the everyday apron and the Sunday one. The prettiest apron was saved for special occasions to protect the Sunday-go-to-meetin' dress. It was usually made from sheer fabric with fancy trim such as ruffles, lace, and embroidery. Some creative women cut pretty handkerchiefs into fourths and sewed the squares into the bottoms of the aprons. This provided scallops and embroidered flowers without a lot of extra work. The Sunday apron might be short, covering from the waist down, while the everyday apron always had a bib.

The everyday apron was made not as much for looks as for practical purposes. It could be sewn from feed sacks, scraps of material, or parts of worn dresses. It had one or two pockets for carrying objects. A bib on top was held by a strap around the neck, or it could be fastened to the dress with two big safety pins.

The primary purpose of the everyday apron was to keep the dress clean. In the days of lye soap, outdoor wash kettles, scrub boards, and zinc wash tubs, a woman did not don a clean dress each day. In the first place, she did not own that many. Secondly, dirty clothes were collected to be washed on a certain day each week. It was easier to wash a few aprons than a few dresses.

The lady of the house found innovative uses for the apron. If she went out without a basket or bucket, no problem. The apron was available on demand. She caught up the bottom corners, and presto! It instantly became a roomy cloth container.

If she went walking in the springtime, she might collect wild greens such as poke, narrow dock, lamb's quarter, or dandelion. She could cook them alone or mix them with greens from the garden.

When it was time to build a fire in the wood cook stove to cook supper, the apron could hold kindling and even a few sticks of wood. Of course, the men should have left those handy in the wood box, but occasionally they forgot.

The apron was chicken-friendly. It wasn't unusual to hear "Cheep, cheep" coming from the bunched-up apron at twilight as baby chicks were transported to be with their mother in a coop for safety through the night.

In late afternoon the housewife loaded her apron with shelled corn. She called, "Chick, chick," as she scattered handfuls of corn on the ground. Chickens came from all directions to gobble up the tasty morsels.

The apron held eggs from nests in the hen house. We could have called it the chicken house, since both roosters and hens roosted there. But we always called it the hen house, probably because hens spent more time there, laying eggs and hatching their young.

On occasion a woman even protected her chickens with the apron. If she saw a hawk eyeing the chicken yard longingly, she flapped her apron at him, yelling, "Shoo! Shoo! You get away from here," and away he flew.

The apron also had warm personal uses, such as cuddling. It was large enough to hold a purring kitten or a whining puppy. Best of all, when the family sat on the front porch at night after a hard day's work, the apron was just the right size to wrap around a little girl as she sat on her mother's lap. There was no greater security than

Altha Murphy

drifting off to sleep, listening to a summer night's sounds—grownup conversation on the porch, katydids in the trees, frogs at the pond, while snugly wrapped in Mama's apron.

THE MATTRESS

Exciting things were in store when I arose that morning. It seemed that life was getting better all the time. We were going to the Durnells' house to learn to make a mattress. We slept on feather beds over straw mattresses, or straw beds as we called them. Actually, they weren't really straw beds, because we didn't have straw. They were stuffed with hay. I couldn't imagine sleeping on an honest-to-goodness cotton mattress.

Feather beds were fine to snuggle down in during cold weather. Our bedrooms didn't have heat, so I slept under so many quilts I could hardly turn over. It took a while to get a spot in the bed warm enough for me to get to sleep. I tried not to move to another spot, not even with my feet, because then that spot would have to be warmed. So on cold nights, feather beds were great.

Not so in hot weather. That wood cook stove was fired up at least three times a day. Mama cooked biscuits for each meal. She usually cooked plenty of cornbread so some would be left over for the dogs and baby chicks. She canned a lot in the summer, sometimes as much as 700 quarts of food. That meant the cook stove went all day and often into the night.

It was almost impossible to get to sleep. I alternated between fanning myself and sweating until I finally drifted off. The feather bed made it even hotter, but it would have been uncomfortable sleeping on the straw bed. At times I slept on a pallet on the floor or even on the front porch.

Mama made the ticks for the straw beds from blue and white striped material. Periodically the old hay was emptied out and the ticks washed before fresh hay was added.

But all that was about to change. The government was helping people get cotton mattresses. Several people were at the Durnells' that day to make their own. A lady showed them how to sew the ticks and stuff them with cotton. They used a big needle and course thread to make a roll around the edges, top and bottom. They tacked through the mattresses in several places. What pretty mattresses they turned out!

Naked Ears

Our first mattress went on our parents' bed. But I looked forward to the day when we would have one on each bed. Then we could get rid of those old straw beds forever.

Most people kept their feather beds, since they had put a lot of work into making them. It took the feathers from many geese and chickens to make one. They could still use them on top of the mattresses, especially in cold weather. But if they chose to just use the mattresses on top of the bed springs, that would make wonderful beds.

Soon all our beds had cotton mattresses. They were not as much trouble. They only needed to be sunned to fluff them up, and turned at times. I felt that my dreams were sweeter sleeping on a cotton mattress, but that could possibly have been just a child's imagination.

Altha Murphy

THE RECORD

I didn't care if the old record was warped. In fact, I was happy about it. I wouldn't ever have to hear that crazy song again.

Volnia was so proud when he brought the Victrola home. We all were. We had never had one before and now we could have music any time we wanted it. He bought it from Haley Brown, our cousin's wife, along with several records. There were songs about everything. Jimmy Rogers sang and yodeled about the railroad. One was about Dapper Dan, a mighty fine man. There were gospel songs and love songs.

All was fine and well until my brothers kept playing one record about two little girls loving the same little boy. They said that was about Bertha Ann, my good friend, and me both loving a neighbor boy. Bertha Ann was older than I was, but neither of us was old enough to have a boy friend. That didn't keep them from teasing us.

The neighbor boy was okay, and so was the song, until they started teasing us about him. Then I didn't know which I disliked most, the song or the boy. Each time I heard the man on the record begin:

> Two little girls loved one little boy,
> He loved them both the same.

I knew what was coming. Finally, all they had to do was look at me and grin, and I was ready to go at them. The song ended with:

> I love him more than words can ever say,
> But love you best, my own dear Sister May.

It seems that the two girls in the song were sisters. In the end, one sacrificed her own happiness to let May have the "prize." I was so frustrated I didn't even admire her selflessness.

I considered the situation, and one day when I was alone in the house, I came up with the solution, at least for a while. I looked at the four big pictures on our front room walls. One was a picture of Papa's parents. One was of Mama and her entire family. One showed a boy kneeling by his bed saying his prayers with his dog beside him. The other one showed a young man and a young woman sitting by a bridge. They were very close together, sparkin', as it was called.

Which picture would best keep my secret? I decided the boy and dog would understand my motive for this scheme. So what did I do? I took my shoes off, climbed on the bed, and placed that record behind the picture.

No one could imagine what became of that particular record. It wasn't in the stack with the others. Strange that it was missing when all the others were accounted for. It was mentioned occasionally, but eventually the subject was dropped.

Several months after the mystery, I was in the front room with Mama and the boys. Suddenly one of them wondered aloud what that black thing was below that picture. I looked up and, to my horror, the record had slipped down a little behind the picture. No one asked me for information and I didn't volunteer any. Let them find out on their own if they were curious.

Volnia found out what it was. "Here's that record we lost," he announced. It was warped when he pulled it out. All eyes turned to me for some reason. I dreaded what the consequences might be, but inside I was secretly happy that the record could never be played again.

I owned up to hiding it, since it was obvious, anyway. But I didn't say a word about being sorry. To my surprise, I didn't even get a

Naked Ears

scolding. Guess Mama felt like I did—it was good enough for them after the way they teased me.

THE SCARE

How could one day be so different from the one before? Yesterday we had run and played in the patches of sunshine and shade without a worry in the world. Not only did we enjoy the trip, we looked forward to the visit.

My friend Anna Beth lived on the forty behind us. She and I, along with her younger sister and brother, Jamie and Denver, went to visit Mr.and Mrs. Albert Bratcher. I believe they were their great uncle and aunt. They lived back in the woods, but that was no problem. They had been there before and knew the way well.

Aunt Ida and Uncle Albert loved children. They had one son, but he was away at college. They treated us like we were special. They fed us great meals, played quiet games with us, and told stories. Uncle Albert joked a lot. When it came time for bed, they pulled a big bed down from the wall for Anna Beth and me.. It had a high, beautiful headboard. I had never seen anything like it. Naturally, we slept like logs since we were tired from the trip. The next morning they let the bed go back up against the wall.

The next morning we ate breakfast and headed for home. It was a dreary day, cold and cloudy, a sharp contrast from the day before. We hadn't gone far when it began to snow. That was no big deal, so we kept trudging along.

As the snow deepened, we couldn't see the lane we had followed the day before. We weren't sure where we were. After a while we realized we were not making progress, only going in circles. That was unsettling, but Anna Beth and I did not voice our fears because of the younger ones.

As the snow came down thicker and faster, we couldn't see anything that looked familiar. We were wet, cold, and hungry. The only sound in that white wilderness was the crunching of dead leaves and branches beneath our feet. The only sound, that is, except our hard breathing and the questions of the younger ones, "When will we get there?" We stopped and looked at each other, silently, hopelessly.

Suddenly, a few feet away, a large gray animal stood staring at us. He seemed to appear from nowhere. We had never seen a wolf, but this had to be one. The four of us stood petrified, staring back in speechless horror. It seemed like forever, but it was probably only a few minutes or seconds until the animal turned and walked away through the trees.

When we found our voices, I asked, "What can we do?"

"Maybe we could follow our tracks back to Uncle Albert's," Anna Beth said.

Yes, that was the sensible thing to do. So we started retracing our steps. But wait —after a few steps there were no tracks, only an ever deepening blanket of snow. Now we knew we couldn't find our way back to the house. So we snapped, crackled, and popped along, hoping for a miracle.

We didn't want to make Jamie and Denver more scared than they already were, but I knew Anna Beth was thinking the same thing I was. What if we wandered around until dark overtook us? No one would come looking for us for hours. The Bratchers would think we had time to get home before the snow got deep. Our folks wouldn't know we had left early. They would probably think we stayed over to wait out the storm. There was no way they could get in touch with the uncle, short of someone going to his house.

So we tramped around and around in the woods, a little colder, a little hungrier, and a lot more scared after our encounter with that animal. What was worse, probably no one was worrying about us.

Suddenly we stumbled into something. "A fence!" Anna Beth and I cried out at the same time. "A fence goes some place," she added. We looked at each other, our eyes wide with excitement. This fence could be a border for someone's property. Now we walked with purpose.

What that fence led to was another fence running perpendicular to the first one. After following the second fence for a while, we spotted a barn and other outbuildings covered with snow. Then we spotted it, a house with smoke curling from the chimney, just like in a picture. It was the house we left earlier that day.

The aunt and uncle had quite a surprise when she answered the knock on the door and four bedraggled children stumbled into their front room. "What happened? You kids should be home by now," she said. As they busied themselves getting us warmed, dried, and fed, they fired questions at us until they had the entire story.

After we ate, rested, and calmed down, we started home the second time that day. By now it had stopped snowing. Uncle Albert walked with us a good part of the way. He turned back only when we were in familiar territory and were certain we could get home without any problems.

That big bed, which I learned later was a Murphy bed, was different and beautiful. But it didn't compare to how good my own bed looked that night. My parents always said they slept better on their own "roost pole." For the first time, I knew what they meant.

WASH DAY

My first memory of wash day is vague, because I was small. We did not have a water supply at home. The entire family went to Cooper's Creek to wash and it was an all-day task. My family loaded the wagon with an iron kettle, three galvanized wash tubs, a washboard, lye soap, dirty clothes, and food for dinner.

When we got to the creek, my brothers filled the kettle with creek water and built a fire under it. As soon as the water boiled, they divided it into the three tubs and added cold creek water to each one. The first tub was for washing and the other two for rinsing. Mama rubbed soap on each piece to be laundered and scrubbed it clean on the washboard. Then she put it through two rinse waters, wringing as much water out as possible with her hands. She spread a few of the small pieces on bushes to dry, but we took most of the clothes home wet to dry on clotheslines.

My next memory is of Papa and my brothers hauling barrels of water from Cooper's Creek to do the washing at home. The same steps were followed there, except Mama took time out to cook the noon meal and wash dishes before finishing the washing.

When I became old enough, I learned to help with the washing. The last rinse water had bluing in it to keep the white clothes from looking dingy. We had never heard of Clorox. Bluing came in balls the size of small marbles. We tied four or five balls in a little cloth and swished it through the water until it became the desired shade of blue. Small children were cautioned not to waste the bluing by playing with it between wash days. It seemed to hold a fascination for them, but if they played with it, they were always found out due to the tell-tale blue left on their fingers.

A big dishpan of starch waited for many of the clothes after the last rinse water. We made the starch by boiling water and flour together, then thinning it to the right consistency. We usually put bluing in the starch also, for the benefit of the white clothes.

The last pieces to be washed were overalls, work shirts, and work socks. We boiled them in the iron kettle before they hit the scrubbing tub, since they were grimy from being worn in the fields.

After all this, we hung the wet laundry on clotheslines. When everything was dry, we took the clothes down and brought them inside. They smelled so-o-o fresh and clean after hanging in the fresh air and sunshine.

In cold weather we heated the water inside on the kitchen stove. We set the tubs up in the kitchen, since our hands and feet would have frozen outside.

If we had time and energy after washing, we could use the rinse water to scrub the wood floors. But usually that was left for another day. Some people used the rinse water to water flowers in warm weather if it was a dry season.

After a few years we were lucky enough to have a cistern dug at the corner of the back porch. That was a dream come true. Then the water was handy, just waiting to be drawn with a ten quart bucket tied to a rope. That made wash day quicker and easier, but it was still an all-day job and a tiring one.

Without fail, the next day would be ironing day. One day the next week would be another wash day and the cycle would begin all over again. I began to worry that not only would I have dishpan hands, but washtub hands as well.

IRONING DAY

Ironing day followed wash day, as regularly as night followed day. I liked ironing day better than wash day.

Early in the morning we sprinkled the starched clothes so they would be damp to iron. We rolled each piece into a ball and put it in a basket. We covered the basket and let it sit while we did the daily household tasks like washing dishes, making beds, and sweeping floors.

To sprinkle the clothes, we put water in a mixing bowl, dipped a brush in the water, and sprinkled it on the clothes. Some folks had a sprinkler which fit into the top of a big bottle. They just filled the bottle with water and shook it out. I have even seen women just dip their hand into water and shake it over the clothes.

After the clothes had been rolled up long enough to be damp all over, it was time for the ironing to begin. Warm weather was best for washing, but ironing went better in cold weather. That's because we heated the irons on the cook stove. Our irons were made of iron, handles and all. When they got hot, we used folded cloths on the handles to protect our hands. Some neighbors had irons with detachable wooden handles which could be transferred from a cold iron to a hot one, but ours were made in one piece.

We set the ironing board up in the front room and carried in one hot iron at a time. When that one cooled, we took it back to the stove and traded it for a hot one. We had to be careful not to let them get hot enough to scorch the clothes. We kept the iron moving at a pretty good speed so we wouldn't end up with a big brown spot on a shirt or dress.

Almost everything had to be ironed, starched and nonstarched alike. About the only things we didn't iron were long johns, socks, and dishrags. Everything else was starched except men's work clothes, towels, and dish towels. White shirts were the hardest pieces to iron. Luckily, we didn't have many of those to do.

Ironing was the hottest inside job in hot weather, besides canning. That's because we had to keep the cook stove going all day.

I learned to iron at an early age, beginning on small flat pieces like handkerchiefs, pillowcases, and dresser scarves. Later I advanced to sheets and articles of clothing.

Surprisingly, I didn't mind ironing. There seemed to be an art to it. I felt a sense of pride and accomplishment when I could take a wet ball of wrinkled cloth and turn it into an attractive garment worthy of being worn to church on Sunday. Everything looked so smooth and smelled so good when we hung them or placed them in drawers. Nothing felt better than getting into a bed with freshly ironed sheets and pillowcases.

It took one day a week to wash and another day to iron. One day was set aside for cleaning house and baking for Sunday. Sunday was a day for worship and rest. We didn't do regular work that day unless "the ox was in the ditch," whatever that meant. I used to wonder about that, especially when I heard folks say you shouldn't shove him in on Saturday so you would have an excuse to get him out on Sunday. We had ditches, but had never owned an ox.

That was four days out of seven. That only left three days for other important things. Not to mention all the things I wanted to do for myself or just for fun. No wonder I was always behind. I once read a plaque that said, "The hurrier I go, the behinder I get." That's exactly how I felt lots of nights as I stretched out on those nicely starched, freshly ironed sheets and pillowcases.

Altha Murphy

THE BUTTER

Butter was one thing I had taken for granted, probably because it was always there when I wanted it. But one day as I was churning, I wondered what a butterless life would be like. First, what would we stir into sorghum before slapping it onto hot biscuits at breakfast? Sorghum alone would not be as pretty nor taste as good. Second, what would we put on hot cornbread at supper? It wouldn't be as interesting without butter melting and running down the sides. Last but not least, how would those yeast buns and loaves fresh from the oven taste if we couldn't douse them with honest-to-goodness country butter?

Butter didn't come without effort. The first step was milking the cows. In freezing winter, in sizzling summer, rain or shine, those cows were there night and morning to be milked. If we happened to be late, we heard from them. We strained the milk into crocks so the cream could rise. Or we saved cream from a spout on the separator. Since we all liked buttermilk, we could churn whole milk, not just the cream.

We had a big churn with a wooden dasher. The lid had a hole in it for the handle of the dasher to fit through. In cold weather, Mama set the churn of milk in a pan of hot water, because butter came faster from warm milk. Someone had to sit by the churn and make the dasher go up and down, up and down, for a long time. That could become monotonous unless you did something to take your mind off it. When I churned, I put a dish towel over my lap to keep my dress clean.

This was an excellent time for daydreaming or singing. Millard said, "Altha has a magic tune. It fits any song she wants to sing." Maybe that wasn't all bad. I didn't have to waste time thinking about the right key, just hook the words to the magic tune and let 'em fly.

Every so often I raised the lid and peeked. Finally, a layer of soft golden butter floated on top. I skimmed it off and worked it with a spoon to get the milk out. I put cool water on it and worked that out. As the butter became firmer, I salted it a little. Then I put it into a round wooden mold and pushed it out. If the butter filled the mold, I had a pound of smooth round butter with a flower on top.

My favorite way to churn was to put cream into a glass gallon jug. I shook it back and forth or bumped it on my knees until the butter came.

Some people had a Dazey churn, a glass container with wooden paddles. When they turned the crank, the butter came.

Families who lived in cities couldn't have cows. Some bought it fresh from the country. Others used oleomargarine, a butter substitute. It came in a pound block of white gooey stuff, along with a capsule of orange liquid or a packet of orange powder. They mixed it into the oleomargarine to make it yellow. They could make it look like butter, but they couldn't make it taste like it.

As I said, it took work to put butter on the table. But it was worth all the effort. When we chowed down on warm bread soaked in butter, we forgot about all the work it took.

Perhaps I ate too much butter in those days. I should have watched it closer. Then I might not have ended up overweight in my "golden years."

Naked Ears

THE SACKS

Altha with her parents and brother Volnia. Altha and her mother are wearing dresses made from sacks.

Altha Murphy

Altha milking a cow. Her slacks and blouse are made from sacks. She is sitting on a big enamel bucket and milking into an eight quart lard bucket. Note the saddle oxfords.

It was time for me to have a new dress. So that day I was going to the store with Papa. He would get two sacks of feed and I wasn't taking any chances. I wanted to pick the sacks out myself. I felt that if a man picked them out, he might come back with something I wouldn't be caught dead in. We needed two sacks that matched.

Sometimes the storekeeper didn't have two sacks alike. Then we hoped a neighbor would have one or two like we wanted, so we could trade.

Naked Ears

I can't imagine what life would have been like, had it not been for feed sacks, as all sacks were called. White ones provided material for tablecloths, sheets, pillowcases, curtains, dresser scarves, petticoats, gowns, hand towels, and dish towels. After being dyed, they could be used for dresses and quilt linings.

The items were trimmed with ruffles, lace, and ric-rac. When they were starched and ironed, they did brighten up a room. Many rooms would have been dull and uninteresting without them.

Print sacks were used primarily for dresses and aprons. It took two to make a dress for me, three for Mama. Even tow sacks (burlap) had uses. Draperies made from them, dyed green and fringed at the edges, hung in our front room windows.

Sacks were sewn with twine. Mama saved the twine and rolled it up into big balls. She used it to crochet lace for pillowcases, scarves, petticoats, and gowns. She also embroidered pretty designs on them. I helped her embroider, but I didn't know how to crochet. I thought maybe someday I would learn. That someday came after I was married and learned from my mother-in-law. Some neighbor women who didn't crochet saved their twine and had Mama crochet lace for them. She did most of the handwork at night after all the work was done. She would rather crochet than sit empty handed.

At church or other gatherings, it was interesting to see the different prints in sack dresses. If two girls had the same kind, that was okay. They just laughed and said they were twins. We didn't have a phobia about someone being dressed as we were. It was also interesting to see all the different ways the dresses were made.

I don't know how others got their patterns, but Mama cut mine from *The Imboden Journal* and *The Kansas City Star*, the two newspapers we took. She held the pieces up to me, cut and trimmed, until she was confident they would fit. Then she cut the material to fit the pattern. I was anxious to hear the treadle sewing machine going, because I knew that soon I would have a new dress.

It was necessary that I learn to sew, so I began early to sew straight seams. When I was twelve, I made my first two dresses without any help. Quite an accomplishment!

I was impatient that morning for Papa to get the team hitched so we could take off. I wanted to get to the store before all the sacks were picked over. If there were several kinds of prints, it took a while to make a decision of that importance.

In our home during those years, it wasn't ladylike for a girl to wear slacks. After much pleading when I was fourteen, I got permission to make a pair of slacks. I made them from white sacks and dyed them dark red. I have two pictures of me wearing them, one standing by my horse and the other one milking a cow.

I learned the basic skills of sewing at my mother's side. I was able to refine them under the instruction of Miss Hope McKamey, home economics teacher at Sloan-Hendrix High School. I took classes from her three years, and would probably have taken more if they had been available.

Little did I know that the skills I developed then would serve a purpose in later life. During the lean years when my husband, Truett, and I were furthering our education, I made almost everything I wore and part of what he and our sons wore. I learned that I could take an old pair of pants or jacket and make a neat suit for a little boy. I could also make a skirt from a discarded pair of pants. Well, I should know how. I had plenty of practice on the feed sacks.

THE SPOOKY NIGHT

I was probably ten or eleven years old when Bertha Ann and I experienced the spooky night. Up to that time I had never gone anywhere alone after dark.

Evergreen was a place three quarters of a mile from our house. I have been told that an attorney named Dent came from Memphis years before and built a beautiful house there. It had a dug well with the finest, coldest water for miles around. When I attended elementary school at Annieville, we carried water from that well. The community was named for Mr. Dent's wife, Annie.

Years before, there had been a annual picnic across the road from Evergreen. People from miles around attended those picnics. I understand that my parents attended the picnic when they were courting. I have had old timers ask me about the Annieville picnics, but that was before my time.

The big house was torn down and another house stood on the original site by the time I remember it. Mike and Lisa Holland own the place now and have built a beautiful new house. They had to have

Naked Ears

the well filled in. But even today, if Evergreen is mentioned, most people around here know where it is.

An elderly lady named Mrs. Pratt moved to Evergreen when I was a child. In a short time, she became ill. She lived alone and didn't have any relatives, so neighbors took turns looking after her.

Bertha Ann and I were to spend the night with Mrs. Pratt. If she needed someone, we were to go get an adult. That didn't sound bad at all, since we didn't count on her needing anyone.

It was a late fall afternoon when we walked up the gravel road to her house. We enjoyed visiting with her and she seemed grateful to have the company of two young girls. She had the most beautiful dishes I had ever seen. We admired them and talked until bedtime. We had been in bed a short time when it began raining. Well, I thought, this will make for a good night's sleep. I liked to sleep with rain pattering on the roof.

Sometime during the night, Mrs. Pratt awakened us. "Girls," she said, "I am feeling very sick. You need to go get someone."

This presented a problem. Who would go out into that rainy night? Who would stay with this sick lady who might die any minute?

Bertha Ann said, "You can choose whether you want to go or stay." Neither option was desirable, but after consideration, I decided to hit the road.

No one had a telephone. The only way to get the news to someone was to light a lantern and go to their house. Miss Vesta (Mrs. Vesta Pickett) lived closer than our parents. Children called each woman by their first name with Miss in front of it. I decided to get her. She was the one people usually called on to sit up with the sick or to help when a new baby was born. Miss Vesta had several children of her own. I once heard her joke that when she went somewhere, she carried one, pulled one, and pushed one. But her two older daughters, Montez and Olivene, helped with the little ones. Everyone knew she would be there when needed.

We lit the lantern and I started out. Raindrops hit the chimney and sizzled. Miss Vesta lived just beyond the schoolhouse and across the creek, about a quarter of a mile away. I thought it strange that I had never noticed before how heavy my feet were. Darkness closed in like curtains on a Christmas play. I didn't know what might lurk behind those trees and bushes. I wouldn't have been surprised if something had reached out and grabbed me.

I didn't know it was so far from Evergreen to the schoolhouse. It never seemed that far when we carried water to school. I just didn't realize how spooky it could be on a dark, rainy night.

After an eternity, I reached the schoolhouse. Now, it was just a little farther across the creek. I awakened Miss Vesta and told her my business. She asked, "Did you come by yourself?"

"Yes, ma'am, I did," I answered.

"Were you scared?" she wanted to know.

"Yes, ma'am, I was."

"Well, fear will drive a person on when nothing else will," she continued. I didn't have an answer to that. Without a doubt, something had driven me on.

Soon we were on our way. It wasn't bad going back. It wasn't nearly as far, my feet had suddenly become lighter, and the possibility of monsters had vanished. We would feel safe with another adult in the house.

Altha Murphy

The next morning things were different. It was a lovely fall day and everything looked fresh after the rain. Mrs. Pratt felt much better. After a good breakfast, Bertha Ann and I went home to impress our folks with how brave we had been on that dark, spooky night.

THE COUSINS

No one was more fun than a cousin your own age. I had one named Mary Frances. She lived a mile from us, right past the store. Her daddy, my Uncle Charlie, died while we were young children. That was a sad time for us, since we were separated after that and didn't get to see each other often.

Her mother, my Aunt Pearl, took the children and moved to Walnut Ridge. We missed each other, but when we did get together, we made up for lost time.

I could catch Mr. Rhea Starr's mail truck on Highway 115 at the end of our road. He had a star route and carried passengers as well as mail and freight. He only went as far as Hoxie, but that was no problem. The cousins received a letter telling them what day I was coming, so they met me at Hoxie and we walked the two miles to Walnut Ridge. They also rode the mail truck when they visited us.

Mary Frances and I always did two things whether we were at my house or hers. We each had a stash of paper dolls cut from the Sears Roebuck catalog. We stored them in boxes and played with them for hours on end.

The other activity was playing jacks. She knew all the different games with jacks and was she ever good! I never beat her, but that didn't stop me from trying.

When Mary Frances visited me, she enjoyed doing country things. We fed the chickens and gathered eggs. We played in the hayloft and sometimes jumped out. One summer she chopped cotton with me. That wasn't fun, but we made the best of it, talking and laughing as we went down the rows.

Another time we decided to sleep in the barn. We spread a quilt on the hay and talked and giggled a while. After we got quiet, we noticed how hot it was in the barn. It was scary out there all alone. While the night was still young, we crept back into the house and settled down in my bed. Doors were never locked, and my parents heard us come in. That was just what they expected.

When I visited Mary Frances, I found life different from what I was accustomed to. First, there were more children to play with. Jessie, her sister, was too big to play with us, but her brothers, Charles and Levi, and neighbor kids played with us. Early in the morning,

Naked Ears

Mary Frances gave a sharp whistle, and kids came from all directions. We played all day, stopping only long enough to eat.

Her church was also different. Her family went to the Presbyterian Church. I was impressed that her Sunday School class had a room all its own. My family went to church in the Annieville schoolhouse. There the children met in one corner of the big downstairs room in the card class. Pleasant Grove Baptist Church had been located in the woods a few miles away, but it had burned. As long as I could remember, the church met in the schoolhouse. Other folks besides Baptists worshipped there, too. My parents weren't Baptists, but that's where we attended.

On one visit to Walnut Ridge, I had a new experience. Even though Aunt Pearl was a widow with four children, and it was the middle of the Great Depression, she scraped up money for us kids to take in a movie. I had heard of movies, but had never seen one.

After playing all day, we cleaned up and walked down Main Street to the Sharum Theater. We bought tickets and went right in. It was so dark inside a fellow had to help us find seats.

Soon the action began. Right in front of us, cowboys were decked out in boots, bandannas, chaps, spurs, and guns in holsters. They boiled coffee in a pot over an open fire and drank from tin cups. They herded cattle and caught calves with lariats. They heated branding irons in the fire and branded the calves. I felt sorry for the poor bawling things and hid my eyes when I saw what was going on. The cowboys even took a shot or two at some bad guys who tried to rustle their cows.

So that was a movie. After I went home, I could close my eyes and remember what it was like. I hoped to see another one sometime. I spent the next few months looking forward to another visit with my city cousins.

THE PERMANENT

If only I had been born with curls. Then I wouldn't have had to go through such a grueling experience getting them.

We lived in the foothills of the Ozarks and were just emerging from the Great Depression. I didn't know what that meant, except I heard grownup talk about hard times. I didn't remember when times had been better, and my friends and relatives all lived like we did.

Most of the girls I played with were a year or two older than I was. That's just the way our community was made up. Several of those girls had curly hair, and not because they were born with it. No, Siree! They had help from the lady at the beauty shop. It completely changed their looks, as well as the way others, including me, looked at them.

When I looked at my friends' heads, then back at mine, I just knew something must be done about my fine, straight, fly-away hair. Each time I combed it, it followed the comb several inches up into the air, crackling as it went. It even did it when I took my cap off. If it was dark, it not only crackled, but sparkled a bit.

I didn't want to be the only girl around without curls, so I began coaxing my parents to let me get a permanent. It was called a croconole wave. Money was tight, and a dollar for a permanent was not at the top of their priority list. But I was the baby of the family and the only girl, so eventually they relented. We lived six miles from Ravenden, where that beauty shop lady performed her magic. My permanent did not warrant a special trip, but Mama promised, "The next time your papa has to go to Ravenden, you can go along."

After what seemed an eternity, the fateful day arrived. I was so excited I could hardly wait for Papa to get the team hitched. Climbing onto the seat, which was a board laid across the sides of the wagon bed, he tapped the horses' rumps lightly and said, "Get up!" It wouldn't be long now.

Along the way, thoughts zoomed through my head. What would it be like? Would it hurt? How would I look? Would people recognize me? On another day I might have complained about the hot weather, the dusty road, or the hard wagon seat. Not today! Nothing could dampen my spirits on this, my day to be transformed.

Upon arriving at Ravenden, we left the team and wagon at the edge of town. I felt as if I were floating on clouds as we walked up the gravel road to the shop where the lady performed her magic.

She began by washing and trimming my hair. Next, she soaked it in some bad-smelling solution and rolled it on small rollers. Then she put me in a straight chair near a funny-looking contraption. Several cords were attached to a big ring. Each cord had a clip on the end. She fastened a clip to each roller and turned on electricity. I thought the solution smelled bad before, but it smelled even worse when the heat hit it.

The rollers got warm, warmer, then just plain hot. I was to let her know if one got too hot by pointing at it. She took a fan and fanned where I pointed. Sometimes I pointed with both hands at once.

Sitting there all wired up, steaming in the heat and the stink, I wondered why I had allowed myself to get into this mess. Would curls be worth all this bother? Why hadn't my friends warned me? Well, I decided what was done, was done, and there was no turning back at that point.

At last the lady turned off the heat and removed the clips. She took the rollers out, rinsed my hair a few times, and combed it. When she sat me in front of a mirror, I hardly recognized myself. Did I ever have curls! Everywhere I felt on my head, there were little corkscrew ringlets.

Even after my hair dried, it didn't smell good. In all honesty, it smelled terrible. I hoped it would get better after a few washings. It did.

Now I knew why my friends hadn't warned me about the hassle. It was worth it! It must be written somewhere that if a girl is to look her best, there is a heavy price to pay. When that permanent grew out, I was ready for another one. Having been introduced to the world of curls, how could I ever do without them?

THE TREATS

We had never gone hungry. There was always food on the table at mealtime. That doesn't mean I always liked everything on the table. If something was there I didn't like, I just filled up on other food and didn't complain. It wouldn't have done any good, anyway. We came to the table when we were called, and ate our meals. If we failed to come, we didn't get another chance until the next meal. We didn't put more than one food on our plates at the time. We ate one food, then put another one on the plate and ate it.

The whole family worked hard to provide our food. We grew almost everything we ate; hogs and chickens for meat, fruits, and vegetables. We had sorghum, lard, milk, butter, and eggs. The only food we bought were those items we couldn't grow, such as flour, meal, sugar, and coffee. But at times I got tired of eating the same kinds of food over and over and wished for something really different.

However, life did not always go in a rut. There were bright spots, even for a farm family in the middle of a depression. If, by some chance a little extra money came along, we had special treats. On those days I forgot all about those humdrum meals of other days.

A pound of chunk bologna and a loaf of light bread made a wonderful meal. Mama sliced and fried the bologna. If we couldn't afford a loaf of bread, we ate it with biscuits. That store-bought bread was something else. The loaf was evenly browned and all the slices were the same size. I liked the heels, since they had more crust.

A box of corn flakes was a big hit. I felt that one hadn't lived until he had filled a bowl, put on milk and sugar, and crunched down on those crispy, golden flakes. Needless to say, a box didn't last long at our house.

The beef peddler was a welcome sight. We couldn't kill a beef ourselves, because we had to keep the heifers so they would grow up to be cows. We sold the bulls because that gave us some needed money. However, at times someone in the community killed a beef and peddled it out in a truck. Papa usually bought a mess or two, and did we ever eat up!

Two treats made summertime special, ice cream and watermelon. Nothing is more refreshing on a hot summer day than a bowl of ice cream. Half the fun came from watching Mama mix the ingredients and Papa turn the handle on the freezer. Just thinking about what would be there when they raised the lid was enough to make my mouth water. Some of the neighbors didn't have freezers, but that didn't stop them. They turned a sorghum bucket or syrup bucket back and forth in a pan of ice until the ice cream froze. That was harder work, but the ice cream tasted the same.

When watermelons got ripe, we put a big one in the yard. The next morning it was cool from being in the dewy grass. We ate it right after breakfast before it got hot. If we had had a spring or creek, we could have put it there and it would have stayed cool longer. But we weren't that lucky.

Probably what made me the happiest was to come home and see bananas on the table. I knew I could only eat one, since we needed to save enough for a pudding. The pudding was delicious, but I wished that just once I could eat all the bananas I could hold, just like they came from the stalk. I knew they came from stalks, because I had seen them in Matthews' store. It was just as well that I couldn't have all I wanted. I would probably ended up with a gigantic stomachache.

THE SAYINGS

Around home we heard things described in ways which didn't make sense. But I learned what they meant by hearing them so much. Here are sayings which were quite popular:

TILL THE WORLD LOOKS LEVEL: The part of the world in the flatwoods where we lived always looked level. But terrain a few miles in any direction was hilly and rocky. I thought "till the world looks level" meant you had been doing something for a long time, or it had become monotonous.

NAKED AS A JAYBIRD: I had never seen a naked jaybird, but I was familiar with chickens without feathers when they were being prepared for a meal. It was obvious what that meant.

NOT WORTH A HILL OF BEANS: One hill of beans wouldn't have begun to make enough for a meal. It might make enough for one serving. So if someone or something wasn't worth a hill of beans, they were worthless for all practical purposes.

TILL THE LAST DOG IS WHIPPED: It wasn't unusual to see dogs fighting. If they weren't separated they usually fought until only one was left after the others turned tail and ran. So I decided that expression meant holding out until the bitter end.

CROOKED AS A DOG'S HIND LEG. Roads or trails were described that way. It could also apply to a person who acted in a questionable manner. It was used to refer to politicians at times. I got the meaning of that, since we always had one or more dogs.

WHAT THE LITTLE BOY SHOT AT: That was absolutely nothing. If you went hunting or fishing and returned empty handed, you got what the little boy shot at.

MAD AS AN OLD WET HEN: I wondered why a wet hen would be madder than a dry one. Then it was explained that when a hen felt the urge to have a family, her body temperature rose so she could keep the eggs warm. If the housewife didn't want the hen to set, she would douse her in cold water to bring her temperature down. That made the hen furious. So if someone were "madder than an old wet hen," he was pret-t-y mad.

THERE ARE OTHER WAYS TO KILL A CAT THAN BY CHOKING HIM TO DEATH ON BUTTER: It would take a long time to choke a cat on butter, because he would be licking and slurping all the time you were shoveling the butter in. It meant there was more than one way to accomplish a task. It came as a shock when we visited others and I saw them doing things in an entirely different manner from the way we did them. Guess getting the job done was what was important.

A NOSE BROKEN OR OUT OF JOINT: What that had to do with being jealous or getting hurt feelings, I didn't understand. But that's what happened to Old Jack when I got Spot, my little rat terrier. It was fun to pull Spot in my wagon, but Old Jack didn't need to worry. No dog could ever take his place. He had been in the family as long as I could remember, maybe even longer than I had.

TAKE A PREACHER'S SEAT: One day a man was visiting with Papa in the front room. When Mama came in and started to sit down, she missed the seat. She said, "Uh-oh! I took a preacher's seat." Her face turned pink, probably because she missed the seat. But it got redder as she realized our guest was a preacher.

BUSY AS A HEN WITH ONE CHICKEN: It seemed that if a hen had only one baby chick, she wouldn't have a lot to do, scratching for bugs. But the way that expression was used, it described a person who was very busy.

FRYING SIZED: If a boy were too big to act like a little kid, and too young to be a grownup, he was described as being frying sized. That term probably came from a chicken that was about half grown.

TWO HEADS ARE BETTER THAN ONE, EVEN IF ONE IS A SHEEP'S HEAD: Some folks said cabbage head. That meant two people could think and plan better than one. They could accomplish more by working together.

FEISTY AS A BANTY ROOSTER: When someone was frisky and full of energy and couldn't be still, that reminded others of a banty (bantam) rooster. The banty strutted around the chicken yard like he was as big or bigger than all the other roosters. In other words, if one acted this way, he was feeling his importance.

BLOW SOMEONE UP SO HIGH AN AIRPLANE COULDN'T GET OVER HIM: If we bragged on someone too much, or exaggerated their abilities, that was what happened. Then that person might get the "big head." I also heard this expression when candidates were running for political office.

ROOST ON YOUR OWN ROOST POLE: We didn't really sleep on poles, but my parents said no other roost pole was as good as theirs. It did feel good to be in your own bed at night, snuggled down under your own covers.

LICK YOUR CALF OVER: That meant someone had done a sloppy job and would have to do it over. I heard that most often after I had washed the dishes.

I suppose each family had its own way of describing things. The children in each family figured out how someone looked or acted when they heard the familiar sayings over and over.

ABOUT THE AUTHOR

Altha Murphy grew up on a forty-acre farm in the foothills of the Ozark Mountains. She was a little girl during the Great Depression and has vivid memories of that Era. She is a retired public school teacher and special education supervisor. She is the widow of a minister and the mother of two sons, one deceased. She lives with her cat, Rochester, at Imboden, Arkansas, within a few miles of her birthplace.

Printed in the United States
116459LV00004B/394-408/A